itton-Brock has spent most of his life studying animal societies
.ding colobus monkeys, red deer, wild sheep and meerkats. In
ase he has learned to recognise large numbers of individuals and
nitored their behavio...   .pr. .ctive success throughout
     /es, providing .   g of their behaviour and
     r response to .'   al _on.   He is the
     of 250 scientif.   . n the . olog. and evolution
mal societies and is currently the Prince Philip Professor of
     .y and Evolutionary Biology at the University of Cambridge. He
     .shed the Kalahari Meerkat study in 1993 and the Kuruman River
Res. ve, where it operates, in 2000. Over the past few years, he and his
te   have worked with Oxford Scientific Films to produce two thirteen-
p   .ries of *Meerkat Manor* which have already been broadcast. A third
s.   .nd a feature film have also been made, providing further insights
i   .e lives and loves of these intriguing animals.

MEERKAT MANOR

FLOWER OF THE KALAHARI

Tim Clutton-Brock

PHOENIX

A PHOENIX PAPERBACK

First published in Great Britain in 2007
by Weidenfeld & Nicolson
This paperback edition published in 2008
by Phoenix,
an imprint of Orion Books Ltd,
Orion House, 5 Upper St Martin's Lane,
London WC2H 9EA

An Hachette Livre UK company

1 3 5 7 9 10 8 6 4 2

Photography by Tim Clutton-Brock
Supplementary photography by Joah Madden, Rob Sutcliffe and Andy Young

The right of Tim Clutton-Brock to be identified as the author of
this work has been asserted by him in accordance with the
Copyright, Designs and Patents Act 1988.

The title of this book is based on the character 'Flower' from the television series
Meerkat Manor, produced by Oxford Scientific Films for Animal Planet.

A CIP catalogue record for this book
is available from the British Library.

ISBN 978-0-7538-2314-9

Printed and bound in Great Britain by
Clays Ltd, St Ives plc

The Orion Publishing Group's policy is to use papers that
are natural, renewable and recyclable products and
made from wood grown in sustainable forests. The logging
and manufacturing processes are expected to conform to
the environmental regulations of the country of origin.

www.orionbooks.co.uk

CONTENTS

PROLOGUE

This is the story of a meerkat. More specifically, it is the story of Flower, the dominant female of a group we call Whiskers. It is a true story in the sense that Flower isn't a fictitious character drawn from all the other female meerkats we have known over the years. It's the real story of a real animal. She was born on 15 March 2000, the smallest of a litter of four pups, and is now nearly seven years old. She has reared twelve litters of pups since she was born and has at least twenty surviving offspring. She goes foraging each day, looks after her pups and defends her position against her older daughters and her range against her neighbours.

It is the story of Flower's birth to Holly, the dominant female of Whiskers group. And of Holly's role in the group until her death, when she was replaced by her niece and then by her daughter, both of them incapable of controlling the other females in the group, leaving Whiskers unable to breed successfully and at risk of being driven from its range by powerful neighbours. Of how Flower was banished from the group by her eldest sister and was only saved from near-certain death by her sudden end. Finally, it is the story of how Flower returned and acquired the dominant position, tried to breed and failed, until, in the nick of time, she suppressed her competitors and reared three successive litters of pups, saving herself and her group from losing their range to rivals, so that Whiskers were able to take over their range, making Flower queen of her group – and of all she surveys. It is also the story of how we have come to understand the complex society of meerkats and the evolution of their unusual level of co-operation.

But before I tell you Flower's story, I need to explain why, together with my team of colleagues and assistants, I have spent the last fourteen years following the lives of meerkats in a remote part of the southern Kalahari. I need to introduce the questions that drive our research. I need to describe how we have eventually reached a situation where the wild meerkats that we work with allow us to watch them from a few feet away, to weigh them several times a day and to pick them up when we have to.

* * *

I have spent my life working on the evolution and ecology of animal societies. Animals vary widely in the way they live. Some are solitary, others social. In some species, individuals are faithful to a single mate throughout their lives, in others, males guard harems of females or mate promiscuously, and, in a few, females guard harems of males. In some animals females care for eggs and young while, in others, males do. And in some cases, a single female breeds and all the other members of her group raise her young. I am interested in why this diversity of ways of living has evolved and what consequences different breeding systems have for the ecology, population dynamics and genetic structure of populations.

Similar principles apply in quite different species so we usually try to choose ones that offer unusual opportunities to answer general questions. We have worked on assassin bugs and tsetse flies, on sea horses and cichlid fish, on manakins and babblers, on colobus monkeys, red deer and rhinos. And, most recently, on meerkats. Sometimes, our work has direct implications for problems of conservation and our research focuses on the application of our results – to the management of populations of red deer and other ungulates, to the control of TB in badgers or to the conservation of primates and carnivores. But most of our work concerns fundamental questions rather than the solution of particular management problems. We don't, for example, work on meerkats because they are rare or endangered.

Some of the questions we investigate are so simple they are often overlooked. For example, why do most bird species breed in monogamous pairs, while most mammals have polygynous breeding systems where one male guards and breeds with several females? Why are females responsible for caring for eggs or young in most birds and mammals, while males are the principal carers in fish? Why are males larger, fiercer and shorter-lived than females in some animals (including humans), while females are larger and fiercer in others? And why, in most social mammals, do females often remain in the same group throughout their lives while males disperse, while in others, females disperse and males remain in the group where they are born?

Other questions are more technical. For example, how successful are dominant males at monopolising access to the females that
they guard and how often do other males sneak in and breed with
their females when their attention is diverted? Answering this
question has involved collaboration with geneticists who have
developed DNA fingerprinting for each of the species we have
worked on. How do females in some animal societies suppress the
fertility of all other females living in the same group? To investigate this, we have needed to work with reproductive physiologists
to develop methods of measuring hormone levels in faeces and
urine, and we can now measure hormonal changes in females
without regularly anaesthetising them to take blood. As a result, I
have become the only bulk exporter of meerkat dung in Africa.
Since each fecal sample is much the same size as an AA battery and
is individually packed in a small coin bag, we have often needed
to reassure the US Customs and Excise that 'meerkat fecal samples'
is not another name for skunk.

If you are interested in animal societies, the complex and
specialised societies of ants, wasps and termites raise important
questions. Breeding groups can be kept in the laboratory so that it
is possible to manipulate individuals and groups and to tease apart
the causes and consequences of their behaviour. As a result, many
of the ablest scientists working on animal societies have focused
on social insects. However, one of the reasons for investigating the
social behaviour of animals is to understand the origins of human
societies and studies of other mammals obviously have more to
tell us about the origins of our own society than do studies of
social insects. Though I have been a biologist for many years, my
original background is in anthropology and this probably
explains why I have worked on mammals throughout my life.

* * *

Working with mammals is not easy. It is seldom feasible to reconstruct natural societies in captivity, and unlike many birds, mammals are usually difficult to watch and hard to catch. Many species are nocturnal or live in thick vegetation or spend most of their time underground. Others are tricky or impossible to follow because they range over thousands of square miles or spend most of their lives at sea. Larger species are often difficult to handle. Yet to understand how mammal societies operate and why individuals behave as they do, it is important to know the sex and age of individuals, who their parents are, who breeds with whom and how group members are related to each other. Think of trying to sort that out with blue whales, or wolverines or wildebeest.

To get to grips with what is going on in groups of wild mammals, you need to be able to identify individuals. The first detailed studies of mammals in the wild got under way in the 1960s and 1970s. Many of the early ones followed large, charismatic species and the scientists concerned became celebrities: Jane Goodall on chimpanzees, Dian Fossey on gorillas, Iain Douglas-Hamilton and Cynthia Moss on elephants and George Schaller on lions and tigers. Similar investigations of smaller species attracted less attention but often generated results of just as much interest: John Rood on dwarf mongooses, Paul Sherman on ground squirrels, John Hoogland on prairie dogs, Patricia Moehlman on jackals, Jeanne and Stuart Altmann on baboons and Dorothy Cheney and Robert Seyfarth on vervet monkeys. Many of these projects started in the savannahs and woodlands of East Africa, partly because Africa contained the highest concentrations of large wild mammals in the world.

The studies that generated the best data and got closest to achieving their research objectives were those working with relatively accessible species that were active by day and lived in open environments. I learned this the hard way, by initially working on the evolution of sociality in red colobus monkeys in the forests of western Tanzania. Unlike the common black and white colobus, which usually live in groups of five to ten, red colobus monkeys live in groups of up to fifty or more. My research aimed to find out why, and involved measuring the abundance and distribution of the food they ate, measuring the frequency of competition and describing their responses to neighbouring troops. The monkeys fed on foliage in the forest canopy fifty to a hundred feet above my head. Until they were used to me, they hid in the leaves until I went away and, even after they had become accustomed to my presence, they were often difficult to see and I could seldom watch more than one or two animals out of a troop of fifty at any one time. I learned to recognise individuals from the shape of the bell-pull tails that hung down below the branches they sat on, but much of their lives remained a mystery.

Most of the time, the colobus were either stuffing their mouths with leaves or digesting their latest meal, apparently asleep, but burping at intervals. For days at a time, they did little else and I dozed below them, dutifully recording the activities of all individuals I could see at regular intervals. There's a tail, there's another, looks like they're feeding on *Albizia* leaves. Or is that one asleep? Yes, and there's another and another. This is getting good, I can see two and a half animals on that branch ... now, no one's active, just some burping. Still no change, and its getting hotter ... and stickier ... I wonder whether they'll have two more bouts of leaf-eating or three before they settle for the night ... God, I'm sleepy, I think they've got the right idea ...

Splish splash, splish splash of leaves sixty feet above me. Yeow, yeow, yeow of monkeys – more shaking leaves ... What's happening? Are chimpanzees attacking them again? Where are my binoculars? Why is everything so far away? Try the other end. Is that Clubtail chasing Venus? Or is he really chasing Pigtail? Or did Pigtail chase Venus and Clubtail intervene? This is fascinating but I can't see a darn thing. Where's my recorder? Why are my bloody batteries flat? Aaah, the tapes have twisted around the spool. Was that Clubtail alarm calling? Oh, it wasn't Venus, it was Cleopatra after all. I can now make out her tail clearly. No, that's Clubtail shaking the branches ... or possibly the Devil ... Now it's all gone quiet and I can't see anything. Well this is really something – by the end of next year, I should have seen at least six of these events. Assess changes in food availability and body condition? Identify which males father which babies? Measure their growth and check their hormone levels? Forget it.

In the Middle Ages, the French troubadours whiled their time away by designing their ideal woman, borrowing the face from one famous beauty, the torso from another, the legs from someone else. Some of their most popular songs described the result, though they were often unpopular with the ladies concerned. Who really wants to be told they have heavenly feet if this implies their other parts aren't up to scratch? While I sat dripping under the dense forest canopy waiting for the colobus monkeys to move, I designed the ideal study animal. Unlike the colobus monkeys, it would do something reasonably frequently. Almost anything would be OK but preferably a social activity that would reveal interesting relationships between individuals. It would live at ground level so that it could not urinate in my face as I peered up at its bottom trying to recognise it by the shape of its tail. Its food supply would be accessible. And it would ideally live in open country rather than rainforest where it was impossible to see much and everything rotted.

After finishing my study of colobus monkeys, I worked on red deer (or elk as they are called in America) on the open moorlands of the Scottish Highlands. In 1972, with Fiona Guinness, I set up a study of red deer on the Isle of Rum in the Hebrides which still continues today. Working on red deer on Rum was much easier than working with the colobus. Like most of the Highlands, Rum had been largely cleared of woodland and scrub by the beginning of the eighteenth century as a result of cutting, burning and over-grazing by sheep and cattle. We could recognise virtually all individuals using the area and assess their growth and condition. We could monitor the mating success of different males in the rut and catch three-quarters of all the calves born to take blood samples for genetic analysis. We could usually tell when animals were about to die and so were able to find their bodies and collect their skeletons.

Like many other ungulates, red deer are polygynous and males hold and defend harems of up to thirty or more females in the October rut. There is intense competition between males. For every male that successfully gets a large harem, there are many that don't, who stand, waiting in the wings, ready to challenge harem holders at the first opportunity. The males that consistently win fights and maintain large harems are generally large animals in good condition. Having big, strong antlers is also important, for individuals with weak antlers commonly break them and are then unable to fight effectively. In contrast, females don't need to compete for mating partners for there is no shortage of males ready to mate. Over countless generations, natural selection has consequently favoured large males and, as a result, males are now almost twice as heavy as females.

Our work on deer focused on reproductive competition in males and females and the contrasts in the growth and size of the two sexes that it generated. We compared the factors affecting survival and breeding success in males and females and found that early growth mattered much more to males than females. Male deer calves grew faster and made greater demands on their mothers than females, and mothers that had reared sons were more likely to die in the next winter than those that had reared daughters. The greater needs of juvenile males also affected their survival when food was scarce and, in hard winters, male calves and yearlings were more likely to die than females. If they survived, the growth rate of males was more strongly affected by adverse conditions. We subsequently extended our work to investigate related questions in sheep on the island of St Kilda and in several species of antelope in Africa, but by 1990 I was ready for a change and beginning to think about what I would do next.

Competition between individuals for breeding opportunities is almost universal in animals, though it is not always as intense as between red deer. But some animals co-operate with each other, even spending much of their lives helping to rear other animals' offspring rather than breeding themselves. Animal societies that depend on co-operation between individuals are found in insects, fish, birds and mammals. The most highly developed of all are found in ants, wasps and termites, where colonies can number tens of thousands. Most co-operative insect societies are effectively made up of females, for males play little part in the activities of the colony and often have short lifespans. In many species, there is only a single breeding female or queen in each colony and all colony members are close relatives. The helpers or workers often perform different tasks in protecting and provisioning the colony and are physically modified for the parts that they play. Smaller castes collect food, keep the colony tidy or care for the eggs and juveniles while larger castes (often equipped with fearsome weapons) defend the colony against parasites, predators and neighbours and play a leading role in raiding neighbouring colonies. The breeding females (queens) are often modified for their role as egg producers and are usually dependent on other group members to feed them as well as to defend the colony and rear their young. In some termites, queens are several hundred times the weight of workers, huge elongated bags of nutrients that are capable of pumping out thousands of eggs a year. In many ants and wasps, workers are commonly sterile and their only chance of increasing their genetic representation is to help related queens to breed. As a result, colony members share a common purpose, and colonies resemble gigantic bodies and the different categories of workers resemble their limbs and organs. In zoological jargon they're sometimes referred to as super-organisms!

Specialised co-operative societies where a single female dominates reproduction in each group and her offspring are reared by other group members also occur in some fish and a number of birds – including some woodpeckers, bee-eaters, babblers and an unusually high number of Australian birds. Among mammals, they are found principally in rodents, marmosets (the smallest of the South American monkeys), canids (dogs and foxes) and mongooses.

Co-operative vertebrates don't live in colonies as large as those of insects, and all individuals are capable of breeding, so conflicts of interest between group members are more likely than in social insects. As a result, colonies resemble families or partnerships whose members often pull in different directions, rather than super-organisms. With the exception of some human societies, they do not have elaborate caste systems and all helpers contribute to the tasks necessary to maintain the group, although younger and smaller individuals may contribute more to some activities while older and larger ones contribute more to others. In contrast to insect colonies, males commonly play an important role in co-operative activities as well as females. Finally, not all individuals that co-operate with each other are close relatives. Co-operation between unrelated individuals occurs in many social vertebrates and is an important feature of human societies. Why do unrelated individuals commonly assist each other? Isn't evolution driven by competition? What do they get out of it? Why don't they opt out of helping? Animal co-operation provides an important challenge to evolutionary theory and so has attracted a large body of research. I decided that my next study would be of a co-operative mammal.

But which? All rodents with co-operative breeding systems are difficult to watch in the wild. So, too, are the marmosets which live in the forests of South America. Jackals and foxes are a better proposition, but most live in small groups consisting of a breeding pair and one or two offspring who have not yet dispersed. The African wild dog and the Indian dhole, Kipling's red dog, are co-operative breeders, but have enormous ranges so that it is difficult to keep track of several different groups. The co-operative mongooses seemed the best bet.

Like jackals and wild dogs, mongooses are carnivores belonging to the family *Herpestidae*, which includes six Asian mongooses (including the Indian mongoose, Rikki Tikki Tavi's species), two dozen species from the African mainland (give or take a few since the taxonomic position of some species isn't clear) and five mongooses from Madagascar. Most mongooses are nocturnal, feeding on their own and living in pairs or small groups. However, several species are only active by day and most of these live and feed in groups, probably as a response to the greater risk of predation by raptors. They include the banded mongoose, found throughout the savannahs and woodlands of central and Eastern

Africa; the closely related Gambian mongoose; the forest dwelling kusimanse of West and Central Africa; the dwarf mongoose, which often lives in termite mounds and like the banded mongoose, is widely distributed throughout Africa – and the desert-adapted suricate or Kalahari meerkat.

Watching television one day, I saw the famous BBC film *Meerkats United* featuring the work of David Macdonald at Oxford University on meerkat groups in the Kalahari. In fact, 'meerkat' is actually Afrikaans for 'mongoose' and is used across southern Africa to refer to all of the mongooses – and sometimes to other small burrowing mammals too. One story is that it is from the Afrikaans phrase 'meer kat as hund' – 'more cat than dog' – which the early Dutch settlers applied to the unfamiliar animals they found in the Cape of Good Hope. A more likely explanation is that it was the result of a mix-up. In Dutch, 'meerkat' is a guenon, a monkey of the Cercopithecus family. There is some evidence that 'meerkat' was simply applied to the wrong animal by the early Dutch settlers.

Though meerkat is still used in South Africa to refer to all mongooses, the name has become synonymous with the Kalahari meerkat, *Suricata suricatta*, which is restricted to the arid sandy areas of South Africa, Botswana, Namibia, Angola and southern Zimbabwe. The genus was first classified by the German taxonomist Schreber in 1776 but had previously been described by the French zoologist Buffon, who devoted eleven pages of his *Natural History* to its habits. Buffon describes how his animals would eat raw meat and liked eggs and how they seldom bit anyone.

In French, Kalahari meerkats are still called 'suricates', in German they are 'Erdmännchen' (little earth men), and in Afrikaans they are 'stokstertmeerkat' (sticktail meerkats) or 'stokstaartje' (little sticktails). They are also sometimes called the four-toed weasel, reflecting the fact that they have four toes on all their feet. The Namaqualand Hottentots called them 'hcryky' – I am not sure of the pronunciation. The species name *suricatta* was added in 1905.

Three separate subspecies of Kalahari meerkats are usually recognised: *Suricata suricatta iona*, in south-western Angola; *Suricata suricatta majoriae* in western Namibia; and *Suricata suricatta suricatta* from the Kalahari and central and southern parts of South Africa. However, although all Kalahari meerkats in South Africa belong to the last subspecies, meerkats from the eastern edge of the species range around Port Elizabeth are shorter, darker and sturdier than desert populations and many zoo meerkats appear to have come from this area. Zoo meerkats, who do not have to dig for their food, are also often seriously overweight and so look very different from wild animals.

Meerkats are leggier than the other mongooses, adapted to travelling several miles a day and armed with long curved claws that are good for digging rapidly in loose sand and light soils. They evolved from more generalised mongoose ancestors, perhaps rather like today's dwarf mongooses, to colonise the enormous inland lake of wind-blown sand that came to cover much of the western half of southern Africa by fifteen to twenty million years ago. Around this time, land movements raised the southern margins of Africa and lifted up parts of the Kalahari, blocking the courses of the rivers flowing from the north so that the water could no longer escape, damming the Okavango River to create a seasonal inland sea on the northern border of the desert. Today, the southern Kalahari is still bisected by river valleys fringed by large camel thorn trees, but they are rivers of sand. Some, like the Molopo, are huge, empty gorges baked dry as a bone by the stifling heat of summer. Others, like the Nossob and the Aub, are more open sandy valleys edged with dunes, down which shallow rivers occasionally run when rainfall is unusually heavy – and then dry into muddy pools edged with thousands of white and yellow butterflies.

Between the riverbeds, row upon row of dunes march to the horizon roughly parallel to the direction of the prevailing westerly winds. You see their organisation best from the air, where the waves of sand separated by lighter dune slacks resemble a sea of frozen waves. From ground level, the irregularities of the dune ridges and the thickets of thorn trees obscure the symmetry. Together with the shrubs and perennials, they bind the sand, anchoring the dunes in their place, preventing them from shifting. The bulk of the Kalahari is made up of these 'fossil' dune systems, except where heavy grazing has stripped away the binding vegetation and the dunes are active and unstable. The characteristic red colour of Kalahari sand is produced by iron oxide which forms on the outer surface of the sand grains. In the northern Kalahari, where rainfall is higher, it is washed off and the sands are usually light in colour, while the reddest dunes are found in the south-east.

As I watched *Meerkats United*, I realised that meerkats might be just what I was looking for. They live in stable colonies of up to thirty or more. One dominant female is the mother of almost all the pups produced in the group, which are guarded, groomed, carried and fed by other group members, including males as well as females. They have a well-organised system of keeping watch for predators where individuals take turns to go on sentinel duty. They form chain gangs to dig out the burrows they spend the night in. One for all and all for one.

Meerkats also seemed to be a feasible choice. They were terrestrial and only active by day; they lived in deserts where there was little ground vegetation and visibility was excellent, and the film provided evidence that it was possible to habituate them to close observation. It was 1992, the political situation in South Africa was changing and the African National Congress had withdrawn its embargo on cultural links with the West.

I arranged to go to South Africa and visited the Mammal Research Institute at the University of Pretoria. There they told me that there were no longer active studies of meerkats in progress and arranged to take me to the Kgalagadi Transfrontier Park (then called the Kalahari Gemsbok National Park). The park lies in the north-western corner of South Africa on the Botswana–Namibia border and consists of the beds of the Aub and the Nossob, dry rivers that used to drain the southern Kalahari, and the dune country that lies between them. I drove the 600 miles from Pretoria with a university technician, Gus van Dyk. It was August and reasonably cool as we travelled west through the parched cornland of the Transvaal and into the sandy scrub of the Northern Cape. On the edge of the Kalahari we reached Kuruman, the main base used by Livingstone, where his wife's parents ran a mission, now a prosperous town. After this, the farmlands gradually gave way to arid scrub with widely spaced dunes. There was little or no surface water and the landscape was dotted with windmills raising water from aquifers below the Kalahari sand. Three hours out from Kuruman we came through Van Zyl's Rus, originally the basecamp of an Afrikaans adventurer. There was a grocery store, a gas station and a church, but little more. We stopped to buy firewood to take with us from a friendly farmer, Hennie Kotze. Two more hours and we came to the park gate.

Turning north along the dry bed of the Nossob, we drove past grazing groups of springbok and wildebeest. The Nossob is one of the main migratory routes for raptors, and tawny eagles, bateleurs and martial eagles soared over the valley or perched on the larger camel thorn trees that grew along the riverbed, while lanner falcons chased the finches that came to drink at the waterholes. Four hours to the north, we came to Nossob camp, a wire enclosure encircling a number of trees that provided shady sites for camping and a few cement-block chalets. We unpacked and made ourselves at home.

Next day, we went out to look for meerkats. A French film team had habituated a group to the north of the camp which were thought still to be around. We searched in the morning but at first found nothing. Later on we had better luck. Gus spotted a meerkat on sentry duty on a dry tree and we drove across to the group, who were digging in the sandy banks of the river bed. They were far smaller than I had expected, standing less than a foot high. I cautiously got out of the car a hundred yards away. Nothing happened. Gus and I walked slowly towards them and the guard gave a muted alarm bark. Some of the feeding animals looked up – but they didn't run. We edged gradually closer until we were less than twenty yards away from them. They were still relaxed and continued to forage undisturbed. I was amazed. No other mammal that I had worked with behaved like this – even after we had been observing them for years.

I spent the rest of that day and the whole of the next with the group. They slept the night in a burrow at the base of a dead tree, rose at dawn and, for most of the morning, went foraging for ants, beetles, larvae, geckos and other small vertebrates. One individual was usually on guard, surveying the horizon for danger and giving urgent alarm calls when eagles appeared. In the middle of the day they lay in the shade of a bush – half asleep, but still keeping a wary eye out for predators. They moved restlessly, covering several miles each day before returning to the sleeping burrow at night. They were entirely tame and were usually visible throughout the day. I had found my ideal animal.

On my return to England I wrote a grant application to the Natural Environment Research Council for a project to investigate the evolutionary causes and ecological consequences of co-operative behaviour. Nine months later, I heard I had been successful and was ready to start. Most previous studies of co-operative mammals had worked with very few individuals – sometimes from a single group – so that it is difficult to be certain about the generality of the results. Having learned the advantages of working with large numbers of individuals in the deer and sheep studies, I decided from the outset that we needed to work with at least a dozen groups. In addition, I decided to use two study areas – one around Nossob camp in the Kgalagadi Park, the other on ranch land belonging to Hennie Kotze. In the Park, eagles, jackals and wildcats were abundant and the threat of predation was constant, while on the ranch, although most of the predators were present, they were less common. Returning to South Africa in 1993, I bought vehicles and hired people to help.

Over the next two years our work in the Park went well. We located eleven different groups of meerkats, ranging in size from five to twenty animals. The groups initially ran when we approached, but it was usually possible to see where they had gone and follow them in the pickup, parking at whatever range they would tolerate. By doing this repeatedly over several days, we were able to reduce the distance at which they would allow us to less than a hundred yards. Then we would get out of the pickup and gradually teach them that we were not a threat either. By the time eighteen months had passed, we were able to walk with eleven different groups and had taught ourselves to recognise all the individuals in them.

To measure the growth and condition of individuals, we wanted to weigh them. Most of them became so tame that we felt that it should be possible to persuade them to climb onto scales if we could provide some small reward to attract them. We tried to find suitable food. Mealworms? Not interested. Locusts? Not interested. Nor any of the things that other mongooses enjoyed – minced chicken or beef, liver, peanut butter, or condensed milk. All they liked were live insects. If we dug up scorpions they would eat these, but turned up their noses at all the more convenient baits.

One day in the Park, we had a breakthrough. We had watched the meerkats eating the eggs of plovers, tortoises and ground-nesting owls with relish, so we tried raw hens' eggs. Passing interest but no cigar. We tried smearing the animals with yolk. A deprecating lick or two but no interest. We broke eggs over their heads so the contents formed a slimy cape over their shoulders. They would clean themselves but had no real interest in the egg. Then, one hot summer's day when we had tried them unsuccessfully with hens' eggs, the slimy mess around the burrow entrance congealed and cooked in the hot sun. When the group returned in the evening, the subadults sniffed it – and then ate it eagerly. Adults followed suit. We could hardly believe our eyes – they liked their eggs cooked! We were away.

Armed with hardboiled eggs, we started to make important advances. With a few crumbs of egg we could persuade animals to climb onto an electronic balance to be weighed. My wife Dafila suggested that if we weighed them several times in a day at regular intervals, their gain between weighings would provide a measure of their foraging success. We began routinely to weigh all the meerkats in the groups we worked with: at dawn, when they got up, again at lunchtime and in the evening. By weighing them again the following morning we could find out their overnight weight loss. We became adept at weighing whole groups with less than half an egg to make sure that our activities did not affect their condition. Later on, we found that we could also use water in a rabbit feeding bottle with a ball-bearing valve to persuade them to climb onto the scales.

We developed regular observation schedules to measure their feeding behaviour and social interactions. At quarter-hourly intervals we scanned the activities and position of all individuals in the group. In addition, we watched individuals for twenty minutes at a time, recording all their interactions. When I had set up the previous studies, I had designed check-sheets that required us to answer a list of questions about the animals at regular intervals and we had transferred the results to a computer in the evening. This was tedious and Dave Gaynor and Ruth Kansky, who ran the project in the Park for several years, designed a system where data were collected directly onto hand-held computers in the field. Particular keys were allocated to particular activities so that it was possible to record the behaviour of individuals continuously. The data from these computers could be downloaded onto a larger machine in the evening, saving all the time that we had previously spent in transcription.

Then disaster struck. In the southern Kalahari, the summer of 1994 was unusually dry – throughout most of our study area little or no rain fell – and 1995 was no better. The meerkats' food supplies dwindled and their condition deteriorated. They ceased to breed and so were unable to replace group members killed by predators. As the group shrank, there were not enough individuals to share sentinel duty and the proportion of the time when a guard was on duty decreased. Without a reliable early warning system, the animals became more and more vulnerable to predators and the group's size declined further. Eventually, seven of our eleven groups died out and we were left with four groups in the whole of the fifty-mile stretch of riverbed where we worked.

Not long after this, the Park authorities decided it was time that we moved on. They wanted to minimise the number of vehicles leaving the road and, since lions were common in the riverbed, we had to take vehicles off the roads to follow the meerkats. Moreover, other scientists wished to work in the Park and the authorities did not want to give priority to a study of meerkats, which were not endangered and posed no major conservation problems. They extended our original research clearance but eventually told us that we had to go. In 2001 we left the Park for the last time. We were just starting to get to grips with the life histories and social relationships of individuals and, at the time, it was a bitter blow – but it was a blessing in disguise.

Work on the ranch close to Van Zyl's Rus had been much slower. The habitat was similar to that in the Park – a bare riverbed with isolated camel thorn trees growing along it and flats on either side giving way to grassy dunes that marched to the horizon. However, though there was a continuous network of meerkat territories, the animals were commonly chased by dogs and persecuted by humans and, when they saw us, would run if we went within three hundred yards. There was more ground vegetation than in the Park and they rapidly disappeared so that it was impossible to follow them in a vehicle. All we could do was to track them to their sleeping burrows and sit close by in the morning, eventually forcing them to tolerate our presence. After several weeks of this, they would allow us within ten yards of the burrow but would not let us follow them when they left it. If we tried to they simply ran away, evaporating into the grass and drie doring bushes that covered the dunes.

Grant McIlrath, one of the technicians who was based at the ranch, was particularly adept at teaching the meerkats to tolerate him. He developed a range of reassuring calls that helped to differentiate us from hunters or farmhands who might have dogs with them. In addition, we eventually managed to find a supply of radio transmitters small enough to be put onto a collar worn by one member of the group. After we had caught and collared a member, we could then track the group when it ran away from us, joining it at whichever burrow it went to.

With radio collars, hardboiled egg to provide an incentive and Grant's expertise in habituating the animals, we were able to make progress. Before long, Grant had habituated the first group, Avatar, which later gave rise to Lazuli. Others followed, Vivian to the east, Young Ones and Drie Doring to the south and Elveera to the west. Some groups contained one or more animals that continued to be suspicious of us and we were never able to walk with them.

Subgroups of animals from our initial groups formed new breeding groups. Young Ones was a combination of Avatar females and Drie Doring males; Elveera of Phantom females and immigrant males from outside the study area; Whiskers of females from Young Ones and males from Lazuli, Moomins of females from Lazuli and males from Drie Doring; Zappa of Elveera females and males from Drie Doring; Frisky of Young Ones females and immigrant males. Each group occupied a range of two to five square miles, so the total area we covered increased proportionately.

We currently work with fifteen separate groups, around three hundred animals in all, spread across fifty square miles of ranchland and savannah. All these animals can be recognised as individuals and almost all have now been followed since they were born. When a pup first emerges from the breeding burrow at around three weeks old, the first animal that isn't a meerkat that it sees is us. Pups are quick to realise that their babysitters are not bothered about us so they get used to us straight away and come to ignore us. We are now of as much interest to them as is a sheep to a rabbit: a safe and familiar part of their environment. The meerkats get on with their main concerns of finding food and keeping an eye out for predators and will forage a few inches from our feet without concern. Occasionally, if we sit down and provide a convenient guard post, they climb up our backs to survey the horizon. If we stand up they jump off but they aren't alarmed or particularly interested. By working with them for so long, we are in a unique position to see what really goes on in meerkat society and to collect information that is accessible in very few other social mammals.

Catching individuals to collect blood samples is not a problem. We simply pick them up by the tail and lower them into a pillow case, which we wrap around them. We used to anaesthetise them with ketamine injected through the side of the pillow case but we now use a mixture of fluothane and oxygen, which allows faster recovery.

Soon after birth, each animal is given a computer code which identifies its group and sex as well as its identity. Flower is VWF026, the V standing for the Van Zyl's Rus population, the W for Whiskers, the F for female and the final number being a unique number that identifies her personally within Whiskers. Her latest daughter is VWF104, which shows that we have now followed over a hundred individuals in Whiskers. In total we have recorded the life histories of nearly two thousand animals over the years from seventeen groups and ten defunct groups. At any one time, we are usually monitoring around three hundred individuals.

Our computers can remember three hundred codes without a hiccup, but it is not so easy for us. At the moment Whiskers alone includes VWF060, VWF062, VWF063, VWM065, VWM067, VWM070, VWF072, VWM073, VWM074, VWM075, VWF076, VWF078, VWM080, VWM081, VWF083, VWM084, VWM085, VWF089, VWF090, VWF091, VWF093, VWM094, VWF095, VWF096, VWF097, VWM098, VWM100, VWM101, VWM102, VWF103, VWF104, VWM105, VWF106, VWF107, VWM108 and Flower herself. Flower's mate, Zaphod, originally comes from Vivian group, so is VVM032. Whiskers is the largest group; most of the other fourteen have nearly as many members and, in the past, we have followed quite a few groups that have now become extinct. We need to be able to talk to each other about the animals. Is VWF060 pregnant? I'm not sure. Was VWM070 with Whiskers today? I thought I saw him roving at Young Ones. Who was VWM070's mother? Was it VWF049? No one can keep that number of codes in their head. It is sometimes suggested that naming animals is precious or encourages unhealthy anthropomorphism. For studies like ours, names are a necessity.

Pups are given names once they start to forage with the group, so those that die before this remain unnamed. I've always left it to the people on the ground to give the animals names, so these are largely serendipitous. There are straight names like Flower, Kim and Flo; names of birds or plants like Ziziphus, ones from Tolkien like Aragorn and Shadowfax; from *The Hitchhiker's Guide to the Galaxy* like Zaphod, or from science fiction literature like Belgarion; rappers, rock stars, film stars, politicians and singers. It really does not matter much. The names are just a tag on which to hang the identity of each animal. The important thing is that they should be memorable. Is Rocket Dog pregnant yet? Was Flava Flav roving at Young Ones? You are less likely to make a mistake if you use names.

Though it is possible to recognise individual meerkats by their faces, it is not easy, so we mark all individuals to make sure that we do not make mistakes. Soon after pups first emerge, we inject a tiny metal tag or transponder under the loose skin of the neck that can be read with an electronic scanner. The tags we insert are the same as those commonly used to mark cats and dogs. But reading electronic tags takes time and, for rapid identification, we also mark each individual on part of their bodies with dots of hair dye – their right or left shoulders or haunches, their back or the base of their tail.

To keep tabs on fourteen groups we need manpower. We employ graduate biologists who want experience of fieldwork before starting on a career in research or conservation. There's strong competition for these places and we only take people who are prepared to work on the project for a full year. The project is organised on a day-to-day basis by a field leader who is usually an ex-volunteer and is directed from Cambridge. In addition, there are normally several PhD students pursuing their own projects. One of my earliest students, Marta Manser, from Switzerland, worked on decoding the vocalisations of the meerkats and now runs her own team based in Zurich, sending two or three students to the project each year. In addition, teams of Earthwatch volunteers come from all over the world to help us out during the winter.

Over time, more than fifty people have worked for a year as members of the meerkat team. They learn how to radio-track groups, how to recognise individuals, how routine data is collected and stored, how samples of faeces, blood, hair and urine are gathered and processed. They see how the project is organised and how observation schedules and experiments are planned and carried out. In the second half of the year, they play an important role in teaching the incoming volunteers how to work with the animals and maintain the data sets. Many of them have gone on to do further degrees working on other animals while some have remained for a further period with the meerkat project as field directors.

The system works well and everyone benefits, but there have also been tragedies. The desert roads in the Kalahari are slippery and treacherous and embanked, so slides can easily lead to serious accidents. In 1996, two volunteers working on the ranch were coming back from an attempt to locate a group that had apparently disappeared. Less than five miles from the front gate, they skidded and the pickup rolled. The passenger, Ben Themen, a student from Oxford, was thrown out and died later in hospital. Three years later, another of our volunteers, Anjeli Nathan, from Australia, was travelling back after a holiday and had organised a lift with a visiting student from Switzerland. Midway between Pretoria and the ranch, a tyre burst and the vehicle rolled. The driver was badly injured and Anjeli was killed. The next morning, two volunteers using a motorbike were hit by a car outside the front gate and both were badly injured. Tragedies of this kind leave an indelible mark on everyone involved and cause serious soul-searching about the justification of the work. We kept going – but we are now obsessively cautious. We minimise driving on the roads by volunteers and have extremely low speed limits.

The land we work on has changed over the years. When we first came to Van Zyl's Rus, we rented an empty farmhouse from Hennie Kotze. The farm was called Rus und Vrede (Rest and Peace). Hennie grazed the land around us with sheep and cattle and was a continuous source of help and encouragement. Then, in 2000, he and his son decided to go in for rearing goats and they were everywhere – sniffing around the caravans we lived in, on the verandah of the main house, in the kitchen when they could, in the living room when they had been evicted from the kitchen. Everything began to carry the sickly, salty taint of goat. What to do? We could not move for we had just invested seven years' work in getting the meerkat population to a point where we could work on it.

At around the same time, our neighbour to the north, who owned a ranch called Gannavlakte, decided to sell up and move back to the Cape. I investigated the price and found I could buy Gannavlakte for a sum equivalent to a year's running cost of the project. I raised the money and we bought Gannavlakte. Soon after, Hennie agreed to sell us the house we were using and a smaller area of ground around it. We now controlled around eight thousand acres, around half of the area we worked on. The goats went straight away and, over the next few years, we took down all the internal fences and removed the other domestic animals. There were already springbok and some of the large black and white-faced gemsbok on the farm and I arranged to buy red hartebeest, wildebeest and eland to complete the natural community of ungulates. One of the consequences of the intensive management of game in South Africa is that it is usually possible to buy whatever you want. Ten hartebeest? No problem. They will be with you next week. Two eland? Certainly. That will do nicely.

But this is the story of Flower, the dominant female of Whiskers. Before I start, there's a warning. As it is a true story, it isn't always pretty. Meerkats are cute, funny, affectionate (to each other), amusing, playful, fearless and amazingly unselfish. But they can also be vicious, ruthless, murderous, uncaring, infanticidal and vindictive, especially to weaker individuals. A female's daughters will lactate for their younger brothers and sisters and will guard them at the burrow for twelve hours at a time, defending them against determined attempts by raiding neighbours, sometimes paying for their bravery with their lives. But they will kill each others' newborn pups without compunction and will raid their neighbours' breeding burrows and do their level best to kill their pups and babysitters. This isn't pathological or maladaptive – their actions maximise the chance that they will survive and breed successfully. It's just how meerkats are – and human values are not relevant. Welcome to Flower's world.

Tim Clutton-Brock
20 December 2006

1

BIRTH

Holly was hungry. In an annexe to the underground chamber where the other meerkats in the Whiskers group were still sleeping, she had given birth to four pups. It had been trouble-free, she had bitten off the umbilical cords attaching each of the pups to her body, cleaned off the birth foetal sacs and licked the pups dry. Slowly, first one and then another of them had fumbled their way to the warmth of her belly and started to suck from one of her six nipples. The last pup, a female, was the smallest of the litter and had been slow to stir, but Holly had continued licking and had pushed it down to join the others, where it eventually found a teat and began to suck. There were two males, Thumper and Hazel, and two females, Petal and Flower.

The pups now lay in a heap at the end of the chamber. Holly needed food to restore her energy, but she was anxious and reluctant to leave them. She pushed into the sleeping pile of bodies, nosing them awake until first one and then another yawned, stretched and began to make its way up from the sleeping chamber to the bright light above. Holly's yearling niece, Risca, the daughter of Holly's subordinate sister, was interested in the pups and came over to smell them, sniffing one and then another and finally lying down beside them. Missing their mother, they clawed their way towards her belly.

It was cold and a southerly wind sighed through the dusty leaves of camel thorns, carrying the chill of the Antarctic across the Kalahari and bringing a reminder of winter ahead. It was 15 March and the burning days of midsummer had softened into autumn. When the wind was in the north or east, it was hot and the meerkats rested in the deepest shade they could find as soon as the sun was high, but when the wind was southerly, it was cooler and they lingered at the burrow before leaving on the day's trek.

Lancelot, Holly's two-year-old nephew, was the first to reach the burrow entrance. He paused, sniffing the air, and then cautiously clambered out and stood on his hind legs looking around. The sky was empty and he dropped back down to all fours and began licking his coat. Holly's yearling nieces, Aphrodite and Artemis, were next up, followed by her yearling son, Dennis Wise, and his sisters, Zola and Vialli. As the sun slowly rose above the ridge of dunes on the far side of the valley the six animals stood up, turning the bare skin of their tummies to the warmth.

* * *

The Kalahari is a land of extremes. In midsummer, in December and January, midday air temperatures of 45°C are not unusual, though it's cooler in the shade of the camel thorns. Sand temperatures are even higher, sometimes reaching 70°C so that the sand is too hot to walk on with bare feet, though below ground in the meerkat burrows it's cooler and moister. The meerkats get up before the sun and set off on their daily foraging trip soon after they emerge from their burrows. The heat builds quickly and by nine-thirty or ten they start to search for food in the shade of bushes and trees. By ten-thirty or eleven they are inactive or have withdrawn to a bolthole to avoid the heat, where they will remain until four or five o'clock when the light softens and the heat begins to fade. Gradually, they become active again, and then move off to forage for a couple of hours before heading for one of their sleeping burrows, where they collect in sleepy huddles before disappearing below ground one by one.

Like most deserts, the Kalahari is relatively cool at night, when temperatures seldom exceed the mid-30s. In the midwinter months of June and July, when the wind is often southerly, it is bitterly cold and in the early morning temperatures of –4°C and even –10°C are not unknown. Then, the meerkats get up reluctantly an hour after dawn. They do their best to find shelter from the wind and often sun themselves for an hour or so before eventually moving off between nine and ten o'clock as the sun rises in the sky and the air begins to warm. The air is crisp and clean, and the details of each shrub and tree clearly defined in the cold light, but the land is dry and dead, the trees and shrubs leafless and the grass withered grey-brown. The meerkats have to search widely for enough food, hunting for adult beetles in the roots of the drie doring shrubs ('three thorns' in Afrikaans), low bushes with an unusual three-directional branching pattern. The meerkats are now active throughout the day, though they head for their sleeping burrow around five o'clock and are often below ground by six.

*   *   *

A larger face appeared in the burrow entrance. Argon, the dominant male of the group and the father of most of its members, was now five years old and had been Holly's mate for the last two years. Like all older males, he had developed enlarged temporal muscles on top of his head. He, too, sniffed the air cautiously and then clambered out and stood with the others turning to face the sun, while carefully scanning the sky on all sides. Gradually the rest of the group joined him until only Holly, Risca and the newborn pups were still below. Apart from the pups, there were nineteen animals in the group. Holly was the dominant female and was now three years old. There were her nieces, Risca, Aphrodite and Artemis, all yearlings, three daughters, Zola and Vialli and Aramis, who were all sub-adults (six to twelve months old), and her juvenile daughter, Wahine. The males included Argon and his brother Delpheus, both of them born in Lazuli, an unrelated male, Beetle, Holly's yearling nephew Lancelot and her three juvenile sons, Dennis Wise, Porthos and Athos, who were approaching six months old.

In the sleeping chamber, Holly anxiously sniffed the pups, turned and made off up the sloping labyrinth of tunnels to the surface. Once there, she joined her family and stood facing the rising sun. But she was uneasy, cocking her head sideways to listen to the pups in the burrow and then turning back to scan the horizon. Soon she dropped down onto all fours and pottered away from the sunning group, smelling the ground. She scratched in a desultory fashion in the bare sand and then moved on to the base of a shrub and briefly dug around its roots. She quickly lost interest and went to sniff another hole in the sand. This smelled more interesting and she rammed her nose into the hole and inhaled deeply, flooding her nasal passages with air from the short shaft. Yes, there was definitely something there, a taint on the air that she associated with scorpions.

Holly stopped sniffing and started to dig furiously with her fore-paws, forcing her long claws deep into the sand and throwing it back between her legs. She dug intently for two minutes, until her head and shoulders were below the surface. Ahead she could smell her prey, which had withdrawn to the far corner of its burrow where it waited, crouching against the burrow wall. She dug on until the whole of her body was below the surface, and only her tail protruded from the hole. At last she reached the end of the chamber. In a flash she clawed the scorpion back towards her, rolled it over in the sand to avoid its flailing tail, bit it once hard in the head and then turned it and carefully bit off the sting. The scorpion scrabbled helplessly in the sand – but not for long. Holly's jaws crunched into its head and she retreated from the tunnel, the scorpion in her mouth. Once back above ground, she ate it greedily, keeping a wary eye out for possible thieves. Then she stopped and looked around again, checking her family and the horizon. All safe – and she moved on, sniffing each hole or crevice that she came to and scratching sand away to reveal hidden tunnels.

As the sun rose fully above the horizon and the air warmed, the members of Holly's family gradually relaxed their raised fur, and one by one they dropped down to all fours and began to scour the surface of the desert for food. Soon they started to forage outwards from the burrow in all directions. After digging out and eating a small millipede, Holly appeared to lose interest in feeding and scanned her dispersed family. She gave a low call and then ran off south-east from the burrow. Her two nieces watched her closely and then ran ahead of her in the same direction. Holly gave another, louder, call – half yelp, half grunt – and the rest of the group ceased feeding and followed. Whiskers were off on their day's foraging march.

* * *

When meerkat groups are first getting used to humans, you reach a crucial stage after a couple of months. You can sit at the burrow with them for weeks on end until they treat you as part of the scenery. But if you stand up and try to follow when the group moves off, they run and disappear very rapidly. When a group eventually starts to trust you and to allow you to walk with them, it is immensely exciting. Where will they go today? Where will they sleep? Will they avoid a part of the range where they fought with their neighbours yesterday? Each day is a new story, each day is different. Usually, they move by fits and starts, forage for a period and then move on again. It is not difficult to keep up, but their biscuit-coloured backs blend in with the sand and you cannot afford to take your eyes off the animals for long or you lose them. At other times they bunch up or string out in a line and move rapidly in a set direction. Then, it's sometimes necessary to run after them.

* * *

Back at the breeding burrow, Risca remained with the pups who were sleeping along her belly. Dennis Wise, Holly's sub-adult son, had also stayed behind but was obviously restive. After a few minutes, he ran to the burrow entrance and stared around, then came back down to join Risca and sniffed the pups. Two minutes later, he was back at the entrance. With some hesitation, he started off along the path that the group had taken, smelling the ground at intervals. He paused and looked back and then, his mind made up, he ran off to find the group. Alone in the burrow, Risca lay with the pups, who had grown hungry and were beginning to suck at her dry nipples.

After walking for a few minutes, Holly stopped. Her breeding burrow was located in the middle of a clearing surrounded by thickets of acacia bushes and she was now at the base of the next dune. She sat briefly on her haunches and stared around, then dropped to all fours and started to forage. Around her, the members of her group fanned out and began to forage too, scanning the surface of the sand for breathing holes, scratching briefly at each and then sniffing before deciding whether or not to investigate. Several of the older animals located promising sites and began to dig, rapidly disappearing under heaps of sand and reappearing to scan the horizon with caked eyebrows.

Sometimes the meerkats' attempts to find food were fruitless and they gave up and moved on to other sites. More often, their frantic digging suddenly stopped and they backed out of the tunnel with their prey in their mouth – a squirming white grub, a kicking beetle, a furious scorpion or a wriggling gecko. Lacking the experience necessary to judge when a dig is likely to be successful and the stamina necessary to dig quickly and deep, the younger animals often had less luck. After shifting several times their own weight in sand, they reappeared with empty jaws, looking puzzled. Instead of deep digging, they spent much of their time scratching on the surface for ant larvae and pupae, small beetles and spiders.

*   *   *

The south-western quarter of the Kalahari – Flower's quarter – is drier than other areas. There is little surface water but, below the sand, subterranean rivers flow with 'fossil' water, often several thousand years old, tapped by the deep roots of the camel thorns and other specialised plants. It's not a comfortable thought that the water in your shower may be several thousand years old. What will happen when it runs out?

Recent studies suggest that the waters below the sands are regularly replenished. As America, Russia and Europe tested their nuclear bombs in the late 1950s, the atmospheric levels of tritium, a radioactive isotope of hydrogen, soared, peaking in 1963. Tritium has a half-life of twelve and a half years and is readily absorbed by water so that it can be used to date samples over the last fifty years. Analysis of samples taken from different Kalahari boreholes suggests many aquifers had been replenished within that time.

Just how replenishment occurs is still not known. The sandbeds are too thick and rainfall levels too low for rainstorms to soak more than the top. One possibility is that rain seeps in along fault lines from hills around the edge of the Kalahari or from rocky outcrops rising through the sand, or even through natural holes created by tree roots or animals. Another is that several successive periods of rainfall can force water down until it reaches the underlying aquifer. And a third is that the collection of run-off from the surface in pools and hollows, combined with variation in the structure of the sand, generates local pipes of saturated sand that extend down to the aquifer. There's no reason to think that only one of these processes operates, so it is possible that all three help to replenish the groundwater.

In some parts of the Kalahari there are daily fluctuations in water levels, which vary with the phases of the moon. These subterranean tides are caused by the gravitational pull of the moon on the plates of rock underlying the great beds of sand, rather than on the water itself. As the moon waxes and wanes, the changing strength of gravity pulls the plates apart, causing the ground-water levels to fall, or squeezing them together, forcing the groundwater levels to rise.

Because rainfall is low and unpredictable and temperatures are high, the vegetation of the Kalahari is sparse and many of the shrubs and trees shed their leaves in the dry season. The most abundant grasses are annuals – like the sourgrass, which emerges after rain, growing to waist height in wet years, so that the dune slacks look like wheat fields. The dune crests, which are covered with coarse perennial grasses, are crossed quickly by the meerkats as visibility is poor and detecting predators is difficult.

Many of the valleys between the dunes are covered by drie doring bushes. In places, these are replaced with thickets of thorny acacia bushes. Trees are scarce and mostly low. The largest are the camel thorns with their rough angular bark, which sometimes grow to forty feet or more. In spring, their bare branches are suddenly covered with fresh green shoots and golden flowers that later mature into clusters of grey-green pods. Away from the riverbeds, the dense evergreen shepherd's tree provides deep shade and is a midday favourite for antelopes and domestic stock.

The animals of the Kalahari have to be able to exploit an extreme environment, where shade and cover are scarce, and to cope both with the burning days of midsummer and with the bitter cold of winter nights. Since the region has been arid for many millions of years, they have had time to evolve specialisations. The smaller herbivores – from the termites to the porcupines – are nocturnal, feeding principally at night and spending the daytime underground or in the shade. In the slanting light of early morning their tracks tell the story of their night-time adventures. Their populations support nocturnal predators – including scorpions, which hunt beetles and geckos on the dune slopes, paralysing them with stings or bites; nocturnal geckos stalking moths and other insects; owls, some feeding mainly on insects, others on small vertebrates; specialised insectivorous mammals like aardwolves and aardvarks; the large cats, which target the grazing ungulates and their attendant scavengers, the jackals and brown hyenas that dispose of the leftovers before dawn.

During the heat of the day, many of the Kalahari's smaller animals find shelter and safety under the sand. The termites return to their galleries of clay, the beetles to their lairs in the roots of trees and shrubs, the scorpions and sun spiders to specially dug chambers in the sand and the geckos to more complex burrow systems, complete with escape tunnels. Confined to their burrows, they provide potential meals for any animal that can dig them out. It is this niche that Kalahari meerkats have evolved to fill. Meerkats can shift their weight of sand in under a minute, their long claws adapted to rake back the sand; their reach allowing them to delve far into the burrows for their prey; additional eyelids helping to keep their eyes from being clogged; and their acute hearing and smell helping to track the frantic attempts of their prey to escape. Like many other Kalahari animals, they do not need to drink, instead getting the moisture they need from their prey. However, when water is available, they will drink greedily.

* * *

Holly and the others continued to forage along the valley between the two dunes for twenty minutes. Then, two of the males headed up the side of the dune and the rest of the group followed them. At the top, the meerkats investigated the roots of the tall clumps of marram grass, then Argon stopped feeding and climbed up onto the stump of a dead tree. Reaching the top, he stood erect, balancing himself with his tail, and surveyed the horizon anxiously. He started giving short, quiet calls at intervals, uh, uh. Below him the rest of the group relaxed and fed intently, knowing that there was a sentinel on guard. Argon's call – the 'watchman's song' – was a signal that it was safe to feed.

After a while, a speck appeared above the dunes a couple of miles away. It attracted Argon's attention and he gazed intently at it, ceasing his regular calls. A goshawk? A vulture? A tawny eagle? Or perhaps a martial eagle, the meerkats' Enemy Number One? Argon started to give quiet alarm calls, hoo, hoo, hoo. Around him the feeding meerkats looked up briefly but kept on foraging. He continued to watch the speck as it rose in the sky, giving slightly louder calls, hu, hu, hu. The bird turned in the wind and the sun caught its dark head, dark underwings and pale belly. A martial eagle. Argon's calls became more urgent. The rest of the group stopped foraging immediately and, without looking around, ran directly for the mouth of a burrow at the base of a large bush, where they stood erect, staring at the oncoming eagle. Argon paused for a moment longer and then half climbed and half fell down from his perch and ran to join them. Overhead, the eagle paused momentarily in its flight, performed a lazy circle and continued down the wind. The meerkats watched it out of sight, then one by one dropped to all fours and began to forage again.

* * *

Living in open habitats where they are susceptible to attacks from the air as well as from the ground, lookouts are important for meerkats. About a quarter of all individuals are eaten by predators each year. Eagles are the main enemy – especially martial eagles –

but also tawny eagles, black-breasted snake eagles and bateleurs. Jackals, foxes, caracals, wildcats and owls are also common predators, while, below ground, snakes can be a danger.

Meerkats regularly scan the horizon for themselves, but a sentinel can play an important part in minimising the risk of predation when the group is foraging, allowing individuals to dig for prey without repeatedly having to stop and look around. Sentinels will climb up onto anything raised – scrubs, dead trees, hillocks, ant hills or, occasionally, observers. They give repeated calls that reassure other group members that there is a guard on duty. Marta Manser recorded these calls and played them back to foraging meerkats. When she did so, the animals reduced their vigilance, foraged more intently and caught more prey.

The meerkats have distinct categories of alarm calls – one for aerial predators, one for terrestrial predators and one for snakes, which generate quite different responses. Each call has a less urgent and a more urgent version. When Marta played groups low-urgency aerial calls, the meerkats looked up in the sky; when she played them low-urgency terrestrial alarm calls they looked around at ground level. In contrast, high-urgency versions of either alarm call prompted the entire group to run to the nearest burrow immediately. Other animals, too, have different calls for different predators: for example, vervet monkeys have one call for eagles and a different one for leopards, one of their most dangerous predators. Sometimes they use these out of context to deceive their rivals – when facing intruders from neighbouring groups, they have been known to give false 'leopard' alarm calls, causing the intruders to withdraw hastily.

The amount of time that a sentinel is on guard increases when predators are frequent. When we worked in the Park, where meerkat groups often encounter predators and are regularly attacked, we found that they have a sentinel on duty almost all the time when they are foraging, whereas on the ranch, where predators are not as common, there is only a guard on duty for part of the time.

Sentinels alternate during the day and there are seldom two up at the same time. Individuals are not forced to go on guard and there is no regular rota – but the same animal seldom takes two turns running. Shortly before a guard leaves its position, it ceases to give the 'watchman's song', and when it goes down, another one usually comes up. To check this, we carried out experiments where we held up sheets of plywood to block sight of the guard from half the foraging animals. When we did this, an animal in the half of the group that could not see the original sentinel often went on guard.

In most groups, all adults apart from the dominant female contribute to sentinel duty occasionally, but some do so more than others. Males in their second or third year of life typically do the most guarding, but some females do a disproportionate amount of guarding too. Individuals commonly act as sentinels after they have fed well and need to digest their meal and we found we could generate the same effect by giving them half an egg.

If predators penetrate their guarding system, meerkats will stand and fight, taking on animals many times their own size. The first time I saw this was in the Park when I was following a group close to the camp. The eight meerkats were foraging quietly in the grassless riverbed when suddenly a young jackal that had been hiding in a hole ran into their midst. One moment the jackal was in the middle of a group of eight foraging meerkats, the next there was only one meerkat left standing. All the rest were spreadeagled on the sand, motionless. The jackal lunged at the young male who was left standing, who stood his ground. The jackal hesitated for a moment – and two other members of the group jumped up and joined the lone male, standing shoulder to shoulder with him facing the jackal. All three were snarling, their hair and tails erect. The jackal hesitated again. Immediately, the rest of the group jumped up and joined the three. Eight meerkats, all in line abreast. Eight open mouths, sixteen canines. In perfect synchrony, the line of meerkats ran at the jackal and stopped. Then ran at it again. The jackal was confused and scared. It looked at them, apparently unable to believe its eyes, then it turned tail and ran. One for all and all for one.

Eagle attacks are usually over before anyone has time to react, so there is no chance of a co-ordinated defence. However, meerkats will readily fight eagles many times their own weight if they are on the ground. Groups will also charge secretary birds that stray too close to their pups, snapping at their long legs until they lift off and flap away. Once, when a film crew imported a falconer with a young goshawk to try to get some shots of the group's reactions to predators, much the same thing happened. The falconer brought the goshawk to the group in a pickup and flew it low across the animals while the cameras whirred. The meerkats streaked to a bolthole and stood there, alarm calling and eyeing the hawk. The falconer then walked across and took the hawk onto his fist for another flight. The meerkats stared, their hair and tails up, and moved into a rocking war dance. In a close bunch, they ran at the falconer, biting at his ankles and trying to climb up his legs to get at the bird. With two dozen meerkats after him, the falconer had little option and he ran for his vehicle.

All meerkats forage for their own food and sharing food is very rare, although dominant females sometimes take food from subordinates. As a result, all meerkats need to spend a substantial

The view from my front door: in dry years the grass dies off and the trees lose most of their leaves, while in wet years the desert can resemble a cornfield.

Meerkats sunning on a summer morning, their heads swivelling from side to side as they scan for danger.

Left The dry bed of the Kuruman River bisects our study area.

Above Pied babblers defend group territories against neighbours with regular choruses.

Right Naked mole rats – the most cooperative mammal of all. They can form colonies of over 100 individuals – but a single female still monopolises breeding.

Below right Like Kalahari meerkats, dwarf mongooses live in stable groups and reproduction is usually monopolised by a single female. They are found in less sandy areas of Africa, and often live in termite mounds.

What you don't want to see when you follow meerkats round a bush:
lions in long grass.

Scorpions are a favourite food – though the sting is usually discarded.

All our meerkat groups are habituated to observers and commonly use them for shelter or as guarding posts.

Weighing meerkats in the Nossob valley. Sometimes, when we weighed them, one animal would climb up our backs and go on guard on our shoulder or head.

We found that we could persuade the animals to climb onto the scales using small rewards of water from à rabbit's drinking bottle.

When Dafila sat to sketch the animals they often climbed all over her.

A meerkat group on the alert in the Nossob valley

Colonies of social weaver birds festoon the older camel thorn trees
and can be home to several hundred birds.

After an alarm, a group watches a predator until it is out of sight.

Even during the heat of the day when they are resting, adults remain vigilant.

part of the day foraging and the amount of time they can afford to devote to sentinel duty is limited. Large groups can have a sentinel on duty for most of the day, but small ones cannot afford to provide continuous cover. So, although individual contributions to guarding increase in small groups, the proportion of the day that a sentinel is on duty falls and the animals are more vulnerable to predators. Individuals try to compensate by more frequently interrupting their foraging to scan for danger themselves, with the result their feeding efficiency falls, too.

Solitary individuals that have been evicted from breeding groups are in the worst plight of all and are jumpy and nervous, often stopping digging to look out for predators or other meerkats. Andy Young, one of the students working on the project, collected fecal samples from dispersing animals and used them to measure levels of the stress hormone cortisol. He found that the levels of cortisol in solitary animals were far higher than in animals that remained in the group – though if several animals were evicted at the same time and stuck together, cortisol levels were substantially lower. There's no doubt that meerkats know that there is safety in numbers.

Meerkat groups have another trick that helps to minimise the risk of predation. In addition to maintaining three or four sleeping burrows distributed across their range, each group keeps a network of boltholes that they can use in an emergency. At any point in their range, they are seldom more than a hundred yards from a bolthole. Since ranges are often several square miles in size, groups may have several hundred boltholes.

As they move around their range, several individuals excavate loose sand from each bolthole they come to. One starts throwing back the loose sand at the burrow entrance, scooping it up with its paws and chucking it backwards between its legs. Gradually it moves down into the burrow itself and another will step in behind it at the burrow entrance, throwing back the sand that it chucks to the surface. Chain gangs of six, seven or eight form and, this way, loose sand is passed out from deep underground. Sometimes, there are no animals at the burrow entrance, just a cloud of dust rising from the tunnel, a sure sign that a chain gang is at work underground. Adults know the distribution of boltholes precisely. If groups are attacked while they are foraging, there is little confusion and the whole group belts for the nearest bolthole to get underground and out of danger. Regular scares must ensure that all juveniles learn the location of boltholes used by their group.

The transfer of information across generations is probably important for many social mammals, especially those living in unpredictable environments. When food is scarce or conditions are unusually harsh, the presence of an old animal who can remember a waterhole or a food source that has not been visited for many years may play an important role in the survival of all group members. One day in the Park, during the long rainless summer of 1995, Dafila and I were tracking a small group of five meerkats that we had named the Jackson Five. We had been following the Jacksons for two years and knew their five-square-mile range well, but on this day they left it, heading south, led by the dominant female. We were astonished – they were leaving all their usual haunts and were clearly in unfamiliar territory. But still they kept going and, by evening, were ten miles to the south of their usual range. Here, they found good feeding grounds and they stayed for several weeks. Then, one day, they returned to their usual range and stayed there. I don't know for sure, but I would be prepared to bet that the dominant female had previously visited the area they moved to, possibly during a period when she had been evicted from the group.

When we are working with a group, we try to be at their burrow before they get up and spend most of the morning with them. After they have sunned, we weigh them one by one, using small rewards of water or crumbs of hardboiled egg to entice each animal to climb onto a shallow, sand-filled tray balanced on top of a set of laboratory scales. When we started weighing regularly in the Park, the groups were small and it was not difficult to deal with individuals in turn, but the largest groups on the ranch can have more than forty members and remembering who has and who hasn't been weighed is not easy. Juveniles can become very greedy, jumping on and off the scales continuously in search of the egg crumbs and making it difficult to weigh the rest of the group. Dominant males mark the tray with their anal glands while dominant females sometimes drive away subordinates in an attempt to monopolise the rewards. As a result, it can be difficult to persuade subordinates to climb onto the scales, especially subordinate females that are under risk of attack from the dominant female. Weighing large groups requires great skill, patience and experience.

* * *

By eleven o'clock, the sun was high in the sky and the heat was building towards its peak. On the horizon, the ground shimmered in the heat while the red sand was almost too hot to walk on. The meerkats now foraged only in the deep shade. Holly and Argon scraped shallow troughs in the sand in the shade of a shepherd's tree and lay in them, cooling their chests and bellies. One by one, the meerkats gave up feeding and lay down. Back at the burrow, the newborn pups were asleep but Risca was still restless. She got up and climbed slowly up the sloping tunnel to the surface. Once at the burrow entrance, she paused and sniffed the air. All clear.

She climbed out and sat, staring around. Nothing stirred except for the mirage over the flats. After a long look, she turned and headed back down to the pups.

*   *   *

During the heat of the day, when the animals are inactive, we tend to leave them and head back to the house for a break and to download our data onto computers. When we go out again, in the late afternoon, groups have usually moved and we use the radio collars to find them. This is often nerve-racking, for searching for them in their enormous ranges can be like looking for a needle in a haystack.

Climb to the top of a dune and switch on the receiver. Angle the aerial and sweep the horizon. Nothing. Where could they have gone to? Move on and try another dune. No good. Eventually a small click on the fuzz of white noise coming from the receiver. Is that something? Another click. And another, very faint. Point the antenna to find the direction and start walking. Try again a couple of dunes later. Much stronger clicking. Check the different directions again, for you often get a signal diametrically opposite to the one that you need to follow. Walk along the bearing, with the clicks increasing in strength. Must be somewhere right around here but no sign of them. Try over there, over the next dune. No, clicks are weaker, so back to the original site. Ah, there's a drongo hovering, could it have its eye on a meerkat? Yes, there's one digging intently and another under a bush and another on guard. Why didn't I see them the first time I was here?

*   *   *

By four o'clock the heat was waning and the shadows of the trees and bushes were stretching across the red sand. Holly started to stir, for she was hungry and needed to feed to replenish her milk supply. She dug out an ants' nest from the base of a clump of grass and ate the grubs one by one. Then ant soldiers started to pour out and she moved on. Around her, the rest of the group were getting up and beginning to forage again. When they were all busy, Holly decided it was time to move. She gave a low, whining call, which was taken up by other group members. Then she moved off and the group followed.

I always enjoy walking with groups on the way back to their burrows in the evening. Often, they string out along a game path and start to pick up speed. If you walk behind them, you can see the column cantering forward, stopping while the leaders inspect the ground ahead, moving on again. Sometimes they change direction and you end up in front of them and they come trotting past you, running round your feet, between your legs. You have to be careful to avoid treading on them.

Over the top of the dune, the group paused, but Holly was restless and she moved them on again. Two more feeding stops and she was ready to go home. She gazed back in the direction the group had come from, ill at ease. Was all well at the burrow? Her pups needed to be fed and she could feel the weight of milk that had gathered along her belly. She set off at a brisk trot, the rest of the group lining out behind her.

Half an hour later, the meerkats came over the dune above their burrow. Holly sat still and watched carefully, then ran down, sniffed the burrow entrance and immediately went down to the pups. Below ground, she found Risca and the pups mewing with hunger. She curled herself around them and each pup fastened onto one of her six nipples and sucked hard, pawing at her skin. Risca left them and climbed back up the burrow to join the rest of the group. After a day without food, she was hungry, but the light was fading and she would have to wait until tomorrow to forage. Around her, the members of her family sat watching the sinking sun or, huddled in twos or threes, grooming each other's fur. One by one they headed down the burrow to sleep until only Risca was left. She sat, looking at the valley. Below her, two plovers were calling, alarmed by some intruder. A wildcat? A jackal? Risca peered in that direction, uneasy but not alarmed. The plovers gradually subsided and she got up stiffly and walked back down the burrow to join the rest of the group for the night.

2

FRIENDS & ENEMIES

The first month of Flower's life followed the same routine as her first day. The group would get up one by one and stand, sunning, at the burrow entrance. Gradually, the new arrivals would warm up and begin to forage in a desultory fashion, spreading out from the burrow. Decisions about where the group would go were taken on a democratic basis, modified by Holly's leadership. When most individuals had ceased sunning and begun to forage, one or two animals would stare in a particular direction and then run a few yards and others would join the movement. If Holly did so, then the group usually made a quick decision about which way it was going and, soon afterwards, they would run off on the start of the day's march. But, sometimes, Holly had other ideas and the move would be delayed. Then Holly would give a long, low, modulated call – the lead call – which would recruit group members to the direction that she favoured and the animals that had started to move off would come back and then follow her in her chosen direction.

As the group left, three or four animals commonly remained behind at the burrow, undecided as to whether to follow or stay and guard the pups. Sometimes it was one of their older brothers, sometimes Risca or one of their sisters, sometimes one of their cousins. Occasionally, two or three members of the group would stay behind. The potential babysitters were often undecided. They would stare at the retreating group and move a few feet to follow them, stare back at the burrow and run back again. They would nip below ground, inspect the pups and then return to the surface. One by one they would eventually make up their minds and canter off in pursuit of the group until, on most days, only one was left at the burrow, usually the most obviously anxious individual. Then the babysitter would go down to join the pups and spend most of the day with them, coming up to the burrow entrance at intervals. Very occasionally, all the potential babysitters would leave one by one and the burrow would be without a guard. Then an animal sometimes came racing back from the group to take up babysitting duty. Rarely were pups left at the burrow unguarded.

On some days, the group returned to the sleeping burrow at the end of the morning's foraging, rested and then left again in the afternoon but, more commonly, they did not come back till the evening and the babysitter spent the whole day with the pups. In the evening, babysitters often foraged around the burrow, but the area had been scoured by other meerkats and they were seldom successful. By the following morning, baby-sitters will have been without food for thirty-six hours and will typically have lost a substantial amount of weight. As a result, the same individuals rarely babysit on two successive days and the previous day's babysitter is usually one of the first to leave to forage in the morning.

* * *

Since babysitting has substantial energetic costs to individuals, we investigated how much different animals contribute and the factors that affect the relative frequency with which they did it. Dominant females, like Holly, seldom remain behind to babysit for they are lactating and the energetic costs of providing milk preclude spending a day without feeding. However, they also seldom contribute to babysitting when subordinate females (who are often their daughters) are breeding and they are not, saving their resources for their own next breeding attempt instead.

During the breeding season, dominant females usually conceive their next litter within two or three weeks of giving birth and over this period, dominant males guard them closely, with the result that they, too, seldom babysit. The only exceptions are in very small groups where there are too few helpers to provide adequate cover, and in groups where the dominant male is related to the dominant female and so is unlikely to breed with her. Under both these circumstances, dominant males contribute to babysitting.

Both male and female helpers babysit pups, although females do so rather more frequently than males. Individuals that babysit on their own are usually at least a year old, but juveniles less than a year old sometimes do so with other animals. As with sentinel duty, well-fed individuals babysit more than hungry ones, and we found that, by supplementing an individual's food intake with hardboiled egg, we could increase the chance that they would stay and babysit the pups.

As with sentinel duty, the number of days that individual helpers spend babysitting declines as group size increases and the workload can be spread. In small groups, intervals between days when the same meerkat babysits are shorter, and younger ones contribute more frequently. This reduces their daily weight gain and affects the growth of helpers. In addition, since smaller, less experienced individuals have to contribute to babysitting in small groups, burrow defence is likely to be less effective.

One answer to the question why subordinates should assist relatives to breed rather than doing so themselves is that, if they are unlikely to be able to breed successfully, they may be able to propagate their genes by helping close relatives instead. For example, if an individual has a one in ten chance of breeding successfully itself but can increase the number of offspring raised by its mother and father by one third if it foregoes breeding and helps to raise their young, it will generate more copies of its genes in successive generations by helping its parents than an animal that attempts to breed itself. The probability that individuals will help other animals to raise their offspring should depend on their relatedness to the young they are helping to rear. For example, helpers will gain greater genetic benefits by assisting their mother to raise further brothers and sisters if these have been fathered by their own father (so that they carry fifty per cent of the same genes as they do) than if a different male is involved (and they consequently only share twenty-five per cent of their genes). By the same logic, it follows that individuals should, on average, be more likely to help their parents than their aunts, uncles or cousins. Since this explanation of co-operative behaviour is based on individuals assisting kin, it is usually referred to as 'kin selection'.

If co-operative behaviour has evolved as a result of kin selection, we might expect the extent of co-operation to vary with the relatedness of group members. Animals living in groups consisting primarily of full siblings should in theory help more than those living with half-siblings, or cousins, and so on. Unfortunately, the costs and benefits of helping vary widely for other reasons and an easier prediction to test is that individuals should adjust the extent to which they help to their relatedness to the young they are raising. So do meerkat helpers that are closely related to the young that are being raised do more babysitting than distant relatives? And do individuals contribute more to breeding attempts when the mother is a close relative rather than a distant relative? Our analyses showed that they don't and that the contributions of helpers do not vary consistently with the individual's relatedness to the young being reared. Instead, their contribution depends on their age, weight and foraging success. After these effects have been allowed for, there is no association with relatedness. However, it is also possible that individuals follow a 'rule of thumb' and help their relatives but do not adjust their behaviour to differences in kinship to particular litters. As a result, positive evidence of discrimination in favour of kin supports explanations of co-operation based on kin selection while negative evidence does not sink them. So no strong evidence in favour of kin selection – but no strong evidence against it, either.

* * *

During the four or five weeks after birth when meerkat pups remain at their natal burrow, female helpers commonly contribute to their growth in another way – by assisting with lactation. Older female helpers – particularly those that have recently tried to breed and lost their litter – respond to the smell and sound of pups by producing milk themselves. Stimulated by the presence of Flower and her littermates, Aphrodite, her yearling cousin, now began to lactate and shared the costs of feeding the pups with Holly. Each morning when they got up, both females had dark wet rings around their nipples where the pups had been sucking. Each evening, the group would return to the burrow at sunset. Our regular records of individual weights showed that Holly and Aphrodite both lost more weight overnight than other group members but that Holly consistently lost more than Aphrodite, indicating that she was still responsible for the bulk of lactation.

In the burrow, the pups grew rapidly. By the time they were two weeks old, their eyes were open and they had begun to explore the maze of tunnels. Their explorations took them further and further from the chamber where they had been born, up towards the light and the fresh air that filtered down into the burrow system. Thumper led the way and was the first to appear at the burrow entrance, with his brother and two sisters close behind. For the first time the pups saw sky, bushes and trees. One of my team was sitting quietly close to the burrow after weighing the rest of the group. Their mother and father, sisters and brothers were standing around, ignoring the human – so neither Thumper nor the rest of the litter saw any cause for concern. Observers were clearly a part of the normal landscape and they became more interested in other things.

* * *

Animals living in or near deserts like the Kalahari face formidable obstacles. Rainfall and food availability are scarce, spasmodic and unpredictable. Hiding is difficult and both above and below ground they face the risk of predation. A substantial number of desert animals solve these problems by living in groups, where individuals assist each other in foraging, defence or rearing young. Several of the beetles that tread a mechanical path across the Kalahari sand live in groups, co-operatively storing food during the wet season, which they share during the rigours of summer. More highly developed societies have evolved in the ants which form a major part of the meerkats' diet during part of the year. Sometimes numbering tens or hundreds of thousands, and occupying a common nest, they send out foraging parties to locate and bring back food. In contrast to meerkats, helpers perform different roles as food finders, carriers, diggers or soldiers, and only in the less specialised societies do all helpers contribute to all tasks.

Several of the Kalahari's birds live in stable groups where co-operation is common, though not all are co-operative breeders. Among them are white-browed sparrow weavers, whose untidy nests dangle from the branches of the camel thorns, grey mouse birds that zoom from shrub to shrub in tight flocks, and pied babblers, that live in closely co-ordinated groups of five to ten, feeding on the ground, like meerkats, on invertebrates and small vertebrates. Many of the desert mammals, too, live in stable groups where individuals co-operate to feed or breed, including several of the larger carnivores: bat-eared foxes, which specialise in feeding on termites at night, localising them with their huge ears; African wild dogs and spotted hyenas, which run down ungulates; and lions, which ambush the larger herbivores. In many of these species, groups consist of a monogamous pair and their adolescent offspring and breeders have relatively long life-spans. One consequence of this is that members of successive litters (as well as littermates) are often full siblings, so that average relatedness between group members is unusually high.

The most co-operative mammals of all are also desert-dwellers. Every now and then in the Kalahari, you come across a series of small volcanoes of red sand, a foot or two high, much like gigantic mole hills. These are the spoil heaps of a co-operative rodent, the Damaraland mole-rat. Weighing around 200 grams, they live in groups of five to twenty, feeding on the tubers of desert plants and maintaining an extensive network of burrows. Their close relative, the naked mole-rat from the arid Horn of Africa, is the most co-operative vertebrate yet discovered and lives in societies that have close parallels with those of social insects.

In 1967, Richard Alexander, one of the founding fathers of research on animal societies, lectured on insects in the United States. He described the elaborate societies of termites and tried to explain the apparent absence of similar ones in vertebrates. In the course of his lecture, he sketched out the kind of vertebrate that he might have expected to develop a society as complex as those of termites. It would live in large colonies that were safe from predators so that the life expectancy of individuals would be high. Since colonies of surface-living animals become a target for predators, it would probably live below ground. For a large colony to be sustainable, it would have to have access to an abundant nutritious food supply. He concluded that the most likely candidate would be a burrowing vegetarian species that lived in deserts and fed on roots or tubers. After his lecture, one of his audience came up to him and told him, 'Your hypothetical social mammal is a perfect description of the naked mole-rat of Africa,' and gave him the address of Jennifer Jarvis, a Professor at Cape Town University whose research focused on mole-rats. Jarvis had realised that they were co-operative breeders, but had not appreciated the similarities with termites until she heard from Alexander.

Naked mole-rats look rather like low-grade, pink, uncooked sausages with two large teeth stuck in one end at a right-angle and a puckered orifice at the other. They have tiny dark eyes, short powerful legs adapted for burrowing and wrinkly pink skin. Unlike the other mole-rats in the same family, they have no hair, even when fully adult. They live in stable colonies that sometimes number over a hundred in the arid Horn of Africa and – as Alexander had predicted – feed underground.

Together with Jarvis and several of his American colleagues, Alexander set up studies of naked mole-rats that still continue today. Working in northern Kenya, they trapped whole colonies to estimate their size and composition and, back in Michigan, set up breeding groups in transparent plastic boxes connected by yards of plexiglass tubing so that the animals' activities could be watched and recorded. Their work confirmed Jarvis' discovery that there was a single breeding female in each group, who can live for over twenty years, producing several litters of up to ten or more pups per year. Subordinate individuals of both sexes maintain the huge network of tunnels that provide colony members with access to their feeding grounds and, like beavers, help to cache food for later use. Larger subordinates guard the colony and attack snakes and other potential predators. Workers visit the breeding chamber and defecate for the pups, who feed on their faeces. In each group, there is a single dominant male who fathers almost all young born to the dominant female.

In contrast to almost all other group-living mammals, male naked mole-rats as well as females usually remain in the colony where they were born throughout their lives and breeding males are often closely related to breeding females. However, some individuals adopt a different strategy. When they are young, they avoid contributing to group activities or feeding the young and grow large and fat. They also show more sexual interest in females than most subordinate males. Justin O'Riain, who first discovered this, characterises them as 'fat, lazy and promiscuous'. After periods of rainfall when the ground is wet and food is plentiful, they eventually leave their natal colony and set off overland in search of other groups.

* * *

Since, in many animals, numbers are limited by food availability, groups defend their range against their neighbours, trying to extend their boundaries whenever they see an opportunity. Stand on a patch of sand in the Kalahari and you will be within the territory of at least a dozen social animals. The ant colony you are standing above may only lay claim to a few tens of square metres. The babbler group whose territory you have entered will be larger, covering most of a square mile. The meerkat range you are in will probably cover several square miles while, if you are in an area where wild dogs or hyenas occur, their ranges will be tens or even hundreds of square miles in size.

All around you, social groups – from ants to lions – are busy defending their patches against other members of the same species. Groups often display at the boundaries of their territories, doing their best to intimidate their neighbours and to deter them from contemplating intrusion or an attack. Living in groups of five to fifteen, the pied babblers have a breeding system very similar to meerkats: one male and one female in each group monopolise breeding and their young are incubated, fed and protected by other group members. Territorial encounters between babbler groups (which have smaller ranges than the meerkats and so encounter their neighbours more often) are common. Members of both groups line up for co-ordinated shouting matches that gradually escalate in intensity. They start with a gentle gabbling – 'we see you, we see you, we see you...' – which gradually rises in volume – 'go away, go away, go away' – and peaks in a rasping chorus – 'push off, push off, push off' – and then suddenly subsides.

Meerkats don't have similar vocal displays but say it with smells and go in for frantic bouts of anal marking in the areas where their territories overlap those of their neighbours. At fixed sites throughout their range, they have latrines where they commonly defecate. Latrines attract dispersing individuals as well as invaders and help mark a group's territory. In addition, they may play an important role in helping receptive females to attract mates. For his MSc thesis, Neil Jordan mapped the distribution of latrines in the territories of all of our fourteen meerkat groups. His work showed that latrine use increases during the oestrus periods of females and peaks at the same time of year as male dispersal. Dominant males commonly overmark the faeces and scent marks of females – while dominant females rarely overmark the faeces or scent marks of males.

For many social animals, not only does living in a group have important benefits, but the bigger the group, the better. In co-operative hunters like wild dogs, large groups are more efficient at running down and killing prey and are more able to defend their kill afterwards against competitors, such as hyenas and lions, than smaller groups. For smaller animals, large group size increases the probability that predators will be detected as well as the chance of effective defence. Bigger groups can build larger, safer nests, and maintain more extensive tunnel systems providing access to adequate food supplies at times of year when food is scarce. Large group size increases cooperative breeders' capacity to guard and feed dependent young and reduces the costs of rearing young to each individual helper.

There is another advantage to large group size that applies in most species where stable colonies live in defended territories.

When solitary animals compete, larger individuals usually win. But, in social species, the size of an individual's muscles is less important than the size of the group it is in. Larger ones generally drive away smaller ones, sometimes evicting them from their territories.

When one group increases in size, its neighbours are likely to feel the pinch as they are gradually displaced from parts of their territory. As a result, everyone benefits if something nasty happens to their neighbours, and inter-group strife is common in social species. In many of the ants, larger colonies send out raiding parties which attack neighbouring colonies, killing their members and destroying their nests. Among mammals, many of the larger carnivores, including hyenas and lions, attack and kill their neighbours when they get a chance.

Meerkats are no exception and don't leave the success of their neighbours to chance when they get an opportunity. Larger, more dominant groups commonly go on forays into their neighbours' territories. If they come across one of their neighbours' sleeping burrows, they inspect it carefully. If there's the sound or sight of anything stirring underground, they will invade in force and try to kill any pups. The babysitters guard the entrance to the burrow fiercely, doing their best to prevent their enemies from entering. Since there is usually only room for a single animal in the burrow entrance, they can be very effective. Raiding groups frantically try to dig around them in order to get into the burrow system and take advantage of their superior numbers. If they are able to do so, babysitters are overwhelmed and both they and the pups are often killed.

Some co-operative animals will kidnap juveniles from other groups to boost the size of their own group. Some social ants commonly kidnap young from neighbouring colonies. White-winged choughs and pied babblers will also kidnap juveniles from their neighbours if they get a chance. We have not seen meerkats actively kidnap juveniles but, when groups fight each other, pups sometimes go off with the wrong groups and subordinates usually accept them and will readily feed them. But dominant females are more suspicious and usually inspect strange pups closely, sometimes attacking and killing them. Their interests differ. Few subordinates will breed in the group and the presence of more group members younger (and therefore subordinate) to them will reduce their work load and increase the group's competitiveness. But for dominant females, unrelated juveniles are potential competitors for their own offspring and are not welcome.

*   *   *

By the time Holly's pups were three weeks old, their eyes were open and they had begun to explore the maze of underground tunnels and spend part of the day at the burrow entrance with their babysitter. One afternoon they had a narrow escape. The heat of the day was over and all four of them were at the burrow entrance. Lancelot was babysitting, sometimes scanning the horizon for possible danger, sometimes sitting dozing in the sun. Suddenly his gaze fixed and focused on a patch of sand two hundred yards away. Other meerkats were crossing the patch. Was it Holly and the rest of the group returning – or neighbours paying an unwelcome visit? He waited and watched. The meerkats came on and paused at a bolthole a hundred yards away, but instead of running on to the burrow, they inspected the ground, sniffing at stumps and at the boles of trees. Lancelot was suspicious and uneasy. He mewed quietly and led the pups to the deepest tunnels below ground.

It soon became clear that this was not Holly and her group

returning from a successful day's foraging but a neighbouring group, Lazuli, on a raid. The intruders could smell that other meerkats had been active in the area and were ready for an attack. With vertical tails and hair erect, they war danced up to the breeding burrow. Once there, the leading adults sniffed cautiously at the burrow entrance. Was it a trap? Were Whiskers at home, ready to attack? Or was it an empty burrow vacated by their rivals that morning? Their noses told them that other meerkats had been there recently, including pups. Cautiously, Ziziphus, the dominant female, entered the burrow and began to investigate.

Underground, Lancelot had herded the pups into a side chamber and now waited, blocking its narrow mouth. He could hear and smell unfamiliar meerkats and was agitated. Ziziphus gradually worked her way downwards through the maze of tunnels. Behind her, the other adults of her group packed into Whiskers' burrow, ready for the attack. They fanned out through the maze of branching tunnels. Treading cautiously, Ziziphus reached the main chamber and chose the darkest tunnel leading off it. The smell of pups grew stronger and she could hear faint twittering of alarm. Coming round a buttress, she came face to face with Lancelot at the entrance to the side chamber. The two animals faced each other, snarling. Ziziphus struck at Lancelot's face but he swung aside and her teeth met only fur. She lunged again and missed a second time. Behind her the other members of her group packed the tunnel, spitting and snarling, but unable to get past her to attack Lancelot.

Above ground, the sun was dipping towards the horizon. Holly and the rest of the group had had a successful day's foraging and were on their way back. Holly had already caught the scent of strangers on a stump half a mile back and was mildly alarmed. She was heavy with milk and needed to get back to her pups.

She coaxed the group onwards, her agitation increasing as the smell of strangers on the path she was following became stronger. Eventually she reached a bolthole a hundred yards away and stopped to scan for danger. She picked up the scent marks of strangers on a stump beside the bolthole and her hair rose. She watched the breeding burrow and saw a juvenile and two sub-adults at the burrow entrance. A raid! She stood up, hair and tail erect, and began a rocking war dance. The rest of the group bunched and joined her, in tight formation, rocking to and fro on the spot. Then Whiskers charged their breeding burrow, and poured down the main entrance.

Below ground, Lancelot was fighting for the pups' life and his own. Pushed forward by the weight of animals behind her, Ziziphus was now in striking distance and Lancelot was bleeding from slashes to his muzzle and shoulder. Ziziphus struck again and again, trying to get a firm hold so that she could drag him out of the tunnel and get at the pups. Suddenly she hesitated, uncertain. The press behind her weakened and she sensed that there were other meerkats in the burrow system. With enemies behind her, she was now at risk herself. She turned, leaving Lancelot and the pups and followed the last members of her group back to the breeding chamber, where there was a mêlée of fighting meerkats. Quickly, she chose a direct route back to the surface, followed by other members of her group. Once above ground, they regrouped, then ran back along the path they had taken. Flower and the other pups were safe for the moment.

3

MOTHER'S LITTLE HELPERS

By the time Flower was a month old, she had doubled in weight. The pups were now mobile and active and were ready to go foraging with the adults. The group had been based at the breeding burrow for thirty days and the best feeding sites within a day's march had all been repeatedly investigated and food was getting scarcer. Each day the group had to forage for longer and return to the sleeping burrow lighter and hungrier. Provided with a stable food source, the fleas that infested the burrow had multiplied and the meerkats now groomed themselves and each other more frequently. It was time to move on and reoccupy parts of their range that they had not visited for several weeks.

One morning, the group got up as usual and the pups joined them at the burrow entrance, enjoying the morning sun. Holly started to forage and gradually the group moved away from the burrow, but none of the adults remained as babysitters. Instead, two of the oldest females, who were their cousins, did their best to coax the pups to follow them from the shelter of the burrow entrance. Thumper, the largest member of the litter, followed for a few yards, then became nervous and scampered back to rejoin the rest at the entrance. Their two older cousins moved slowly away, looking back and calling repeatedly.

The four pups peered after the departing group anxiously. Then Flower, who was hungry, ran out to join her older cousins and her three litter-mates followed. One of the older females led them down the path going from the burrow to join the foraging group while the others followed behind the last pup, guarding their rear. Once they had joined the group, the four pups crouched in a hollow, exhausted and anxious. Suddenly, Holly appeared with something in her mouth. She dropped it in front of Flower – a small white grub, writhing slowly in the sand. Flower took little notice until Holly nosed the grub repeatedly. Then she smelled it and bit it gently. It was soft, full of sweet juice, much like her mother's nipples. She bit it harder, squeezing its juices out into her mouth, and then swallowed the empty skin. Beside her, other members of the group appeared with grubs and larvae for the other pups. As the pups fed, their strength increased and they started to fan out among the foraging adults.

Soon afterwards, the meerkats moved on to a new feeding site. Once again, their two cousins, Risca and Aphrodite, took care of the pups, one walking at the head of the small column, one behind. They foraged for half an hour and the pups were fed repeatedly by all the group members. After a while, they began to play, chasing each other in tight circles. As the heat increased, they collapsed in a pile in the shade of a thorn bush. Holly moved across to them and allowed them to suckle and then groomed each pup in turn.

The group spent the day foraging in the small valleys between the dunes not far from the breeding burrow. In the afternoon they continued west and, that evening, Holly led them to a new burrow on the flats above the river, beside a large camel thorn tree. The sand was bare and several of the burrow entrances had been trodden in by eland. A family of ground squirrels had taken over part of the burrow system and now sat by one of the peripheral holes, eyeing the meerkats cautiously. The burrow was familiar to the older meerkats but they approached it circumspectly, alert for any sign of an ambush. Holly sniffed at the main entrance. Were there any unwelcome lodgers? A puff adder, perhaps, or a Cape cobra? A yellow mongoose or a striped polecat? The hole smelled stale and unused. She went cautiously below ground, followed by Argon and the other group members. A minute later both she and Argon re-emerged. No sign of anything apart from the ground squirrels, who kept their distance. Both animals smeared their anal glands on the burrow entrance. All clear.

Other members of the group pushed past them into the mouth of the burrow and began to clear away the loose sand. Lancelot, the first digger, gradually made his way forward into the dark burrow while behind him Vialli took up position. As Lancelot and Vialli moved further underground, other members of the group joined them until eight animals formed a single co-ordinated chain with Lancelot at its head, now many feet underground. The sand that Lancelot dug up was then thrown back by each member of the chain until it formed a loose white heap at the burrow entrance. Out came the detritus of past occupation – the white joints of a dead millipede, some desiccated meerkat faeces and the skull of a dead ground squirrel. An anteater that had its nest in a neighbouring burrow hopped up and began to pick small insects from the pile of sand.

After a few minutes, Lancelot reappeared at the surface, his face covered with sand, and a different group member took his place at the front, others joining in at the rear. Soon, the burrow was clear and the team all came back to the surface. Holly now led the pups underground for the night while the rest of the group relaxed at the burrow entrance, staring at the sunset or grooming each other. One by one they fell still and then crept below.

Many of the burrow systems used by the meerkats had originally been excavated by ground squirrels that lived in small scattered colonies across the ranch. Sometimes, ground squirrels would use part of the same burrows as the meerkats. Juveniles of the two species sometimes played with each other, but adults commonly chased them away. In contrast to the meerkats, female ground squirrels are usually based at a single burrow, though males may visit the burrows of several females. They are almost exclusively vegetarian and so do not need nearly such large ranges as meerkats to get access to adequate food supplies.

The next morning, Holly was first up. She peered out cautiously from the mouth of the burrow to satisfy herself it was safe to come out. After a minute or two she did so and stood, turning to face the rising sun, leaning back on her tail. One by one, the members of her family joined her. After sunning for a quarter of an hour, Holly led the group off on their day's foraging trip. This time, the pups had learned the routine and needed little persuasion to follow the others as they left the burrow and, soon, the group was foraging busily. For the first half-hour, the adults ate most of what they found and the pups got little food. Then, after the adults had taken the edge off their hunger, they began to give the larger and less mobile food to the pups. Their older sisters were more generous than their older brothers – though everyone gave them a proportion of their findings, including Holly. Only Argon did not regularly feed them, foraging on his own to avoid the begging pups, but contributing more to guarding than other group members.

As they foraged, the meerkats attracted a small retinue of birds that fed on the insects that they disturbed: glossy starlings, hornbills, crimson-breasted shrikes and drongos. The drongos kept a beady eye on the pups and were quick to snatch away food items that were not quickly eaten, forcing the meerkats to spend time guarding pups that they were feeding against their attacks. The birds were often the first to see a predator and the meerkats had learned to respond to their alarm calls. The drongos, in turn, had learned that if they gave an alarm call, the meerkats groups would run for cover – giving them an opportunity to snatch food from the dazed pups. Foraging bouts tended to be punctuated with false alarm calls from the drongos. Like starlings, drongos are natural mimics and one pair had even learned to imitate the meerkats' own alarm call.

That night, the group changed their sleeping burrow again, ending their day at a burrow on the eastern boundary of their range. The area used by Whiskers covered around three square miles of dunes and flats. To the south, the dunes ran down to a large area of flats covered with short drie doring bushes and bounded by the road. Their neighbours were a group of two dozen animals that we called the Young Ones. On the east, the Whiskers range consisted of a plateau of smaller dunes, with narrow grassy slacks between them and many acacia thickets. Their neighbours here were Vivian, a group named after their original matriarch.

Vivian spent much of their time to the south of the road and did not often interact with Whiskers. On the north and west, the Whiskers range was bisected by the dry bed of the Kuruman River, edged with large camel thorn trees. Above the western bank on the edge of the flats on the far side there was the grave of a German, dating from the time when Namibia was a German colony and German military parties often penetrated into the northern areas of South Africa. To the north, the Western Flats were bounded by a large dune of bright red sand, the Big Dune. Unlike most of the other dunes in the area, which were covered with grass and bushes that held the sand in place, the Big Dune consisted mostly of loose sand that was continuously piled up by the wind. The loose sand trapped insects, which blew onto the surface and had difficulty taking off, and at night it was regularly patrolled by scorpions which killed and ate the animals that had been trapped. To the south-west of the Big Dune, the Western flats ran into thickets and small dunes and there was a derelict cattle trough where water still ran. The western part of the flats, the Big Dune and the thickets to the west were all part of the traditional range of Lazuli, who were one of the biggest groups in the area.

Whiskers regularly used five main sleeping burrows within their range: two in the eastern thickets, one on the northern edge of the Young Ones' flats, one above the eastern bank of the Kuruman River and one by a large camel thorn tree below the Big Dune. In addition, they had three other burrows that they used irregularly, and also sometimes slept in one of the larger boltholes. When they were not breeding, the group might change sleeping burrows each night, especially if they had not foraged successfully during the day. More commonly, they spent two or three nights at a sleeping burrow before moving on.

*   *   *

In the morning, the group got up one by one and sunned as usual. Holly started to forage close to the burrow and then began to lead the group off. Behind her, the meerkats formed a loose line with the pups bringing up the rear. Thumper, the largest pup, was first, followed by his brother Hazel, Petal and finally Flower. The group moved fast and the pups struggled to keep up. Flower, the smallest, got left behind and Vialli, her adolescent sister, came back for her and picked her up in her mouth and carried her to where the group was foraging. After a while, the group moved on and again Flower and Petal lagged behind. Flower tried desperately to keep up but was unable to manage the pace of the adults. She lagged further and further behind, giving plaintive lost calls. She lost sight of the other animals and her distress increased.

A hundred yards ahead, Vialli was encouraging Petal to keep up with the group, who were now two hundred yards further on. She heard Flower's lost calls and left Petal, who sat down in a hollow. She ran back along the path she had followed and, rounding a thorn bush, found Flower sitting still and calling plaintively. She picked Flower up once again and set off back to find Petal, who was now running back towards her. When she was still fifty yards away, there was suddenly a swirl of wings and a blur of grey and black blotted out their view. Vialli stopped short, and dropped Flower, who crouched under her belly. Twenty feet above them Petal was crying unhappily in the claws of a pale chanting goshawk. While the two meerkats watched, the bird lifted over the tree tops and flapped lazily away over the nearest dune. Petal's cries gradually faded.

Vialli stood on all fours with tail and fur up while Flower cowered below her. Then she made up her mind, reached down, picked up Flower in her mouth and galloped ahead to where the group was foraging. After she had rejoined them, she relaxed and began to search for food. Risca came up with a large grub and dropped it in front of Flower, who smelled it suspiciously and then bolted it down. No one noticed the disappearance of Petal.

Meerkat pups are frequently taken by predators in the first days of their foraging trips. Pups often find it difficult to keep up and rest alone or in small groups under bushes or in boltholes. When they are left on their own, they give loud, repeated calls and the adults go back to them and either encourage them to move along or, sometimes, pick them up and carry them back to the group. But pups can become separated and then, if there is a sudden predator alarm and all the group rush to the nearest bolt-hole, they remain parted from the others. If they are not heard when the group reassembles, they are likely to be left behind, for meerkats do not appear to be able to count and, even if they could do so, it would be difficult for any one member of the group to keep track of all the pups. Without the adults to protect and feed them, pups do not last long. Pale chanting goshawks are a common predator of pups, but kestrels, lanner falcons, eagles, yellow mongooses, striped polecats, foxes and jackals will all readily take a solitary pup. When pups were abandoned, it was often difficult to resist the urge to rescue them. However, if we returned them to the group, we would have been interfering with exactly the ecological process that we were studying, while if we took them back and raised them, we would rapidly have had a meerkat orphanage on our hands.

The meerkats spent the middle of the day in the shade of a gnarled shepherd's tree, where a hole led deep into the root stock. As midday passed and the heat began to fade, they once again became active. Holly moved round the group, stimulating them into movement. She set off down a gently sandy slope leading to the dry bed of the Kuruman River. Here the grass was short and visibility was good – though the tall camel thorns on either side of the river could house predators. Holly walked out onto the open flats, moving cautiously and giving regular calls to reassure other group members. The rest of the group followed her and spread out to dig for prey.

Many of the camel thorns along the riverbed are home to colonies of social weaver birds whose enormous communal nests hang below the trees' branches, made of coarse thatch. Their societies are quite different from those of the meekats for, although they forage in tight groups, each social weaver colony consists of many breeding pairs, each with its separate nest in the mushroom-shaped canopy of the communal nest. Every morning, the weavers collect on the ground below the nest, spasmodically searching for food. Then, with a whirr of wings, the groups leave on their daily foraging trip, flying low over the dunes in a compact ball. Like the meerkats, they return by late afternoon and socialise around the base of the tree – and then fly up into their separate nest holes.

The social weaver colonies are home to other animals. Pygmy falcons breed in the disused weaver nests, leaving a telltale smear of white, calcified droppings below their nest. The smallest of all falcons, they are little larger than the weavers themselves and feed principally on insects. In the morning, pairs take up position at the apex of the camel thorn and males serenade their partners with a repeated bubbling call, accompanied by rhythmic head-bobbing. Cape cobras also live in the social weaver colonies, using their long bodies to reach deep into the nest holes of the weavers to eat their chicks or take a brooding adult. By day, they are often draped over the canopy of the nest or lying along one of the main branches of the tree.

Groups of pied babblers also hold territories along the riverbed.

In contrast to the weavers, they breed in groups rather than colonies. Their groups are smaller than those of meerkats, but their breeding system is similar. In each group there is a single dominant breeding female and a single dominant male who are the parents of almost all the young. Like the meerkats, babblers breed several times per season.The first brood of the season is incubated, guarded and fed by all members of the group but, once they have fledged, the breeding adults leave them to the care of the helpers and begin their second nest, playing a larger part in rearing their young themselves while the helpers continue to care for the previous brood.

*   *   *

After foraging for half an hour in the short grass of the riverbed, Holly and the others moved up the far bank through the long shadows cast by the camel thorns. At the top they came to a large flat of stunted drie doring bushes and coarse, tufted grass. To the north, the Big Dune was bright red in the afternoon light. The flats provided good visibility and the group spread out and foraged busily. Flower followed Holly closely, calling frequently. Her mother sniffed at a hole in the sand and began to dig rapidly, heaping up the sand behind her. She burrowed into the hole until only her tail was left above the surface. Flower waited but kept calling. Suddenly, there was a pause and then Holly backed out of the hole, a small gecko, sandy-coloured on the back with a white belly, in her jaws. She bit it quickly in the head and dropped it in front of Flower while it was still writhing. Flower's calls became louder and faster and she eyed it with interest, but she was not used to food like this and was clearly uncertain. Holly nosed the dead gecko towards Flower, who sniffed it, bit it and then began to eat it greedily while Holly moved on.

By the time Flower had finished the gecko, Holly had been joined by Thumper and was digging busily behind a bush. Flower tried to join Holly, too, but Thumper rushed towards her indignantly and drove her away. A few yards away, Aphrodite was digging a hole at the base of a drie doring bush and Flower ran to her, calling for attention. Aphrodite continued to dig and found an ants' nest; she picked out the workers and ate the pupae they were guarding but the ants were too small to pass to Flower, who kept begging but got nothing.

Aphrodite moved on, with Flower trotting behind her and calling. She sniffed at another hole in the sand and then began to dig. After a couple of minutes she backed out with a small scorpion in her mouth. Like Holly, she quickly killed it and bit off its sting, then dropped it in front of Flower, who ate it rapidly. Once again, Aphrodite moved on and, when she had finished the scorpion, Flower joined Lancelot, who gave her a beetle larva. Then she went back to Holly again. Her brother and sister also fed from different group members and got left behind as they progressed, and then started begging from the next individuals. When pups were tailing an adult they would fiercely defend the adult they were with from other pups and battles often ensued. 'Owners' usually won these fights, chasing away pups that tried to join them.

The group spent that evening at a large sandy burrow on the flats beneath the Big Dune, close to a single camel thorn. There was a colony of white-browed sparrow weavers in the thorn tree behind. As the meerkats foraged around the burrow before settling down for the night, the sparrow weavers flew down and fed among them, picking up seeds and insects from the piles of sand that the meerkats left.

The next morning the group sunned and set off along the flats to the base of the Big Dune. They skirted the dune and climbed up through sparse grass to the marram grass growing on its shoulder. When they reached the top, Holly stood and scanned for danger and then dropped down and began to feed while around her, the rest of the group spread out. Vialli climbed a bush and went on guard. After they had foraged for ten minutes, they were suddenly alerted by an alarm call from Risca, who was staring across the thorn scrub that covered the back of the Big Dune. There were other meerkats there.

The Whiskers bunched and peered ahead towards the other group, their hair on end and their tails erect. Holly and Argon started a rocking war dance on the spot and the others gradually joined in. Soon the whole group was rocking to and fro from their front legs to their hind legs and back again. The other group had seen them and were also war dancing a hundred yards away. Risca continued to give alarm calls and the other group members did so too. Suddenly, as if a trigger had been pulled, Whiskers charged, bounding over the sand in an exaggerated fashion. The pups held back, drawing close to Vialli and Zola, her sister, who remained behind.

The two groups met and individuals on both sides chased or bit at each other. Holly confronted and then chased a female, while Argon sparred with two big males. Athos, Flower's yearling brother, went down with two males biting at him while Porthos, his litter-mate, chased a sub-adult away. In the middle was a large female, snapping at all comers. Their opponents were Lazuli, the group whose range lay to the north of theirs, and Whiskers were clearly outnumbered. Eventually Holly broke off and the two groups gradually drew apart, still war dancing. Holly turned, dropped her tail and ran back towards where Zola, Vialli and the pups were watching. Behind her, the rest of the group followed her lead. They ran halfway back across the flats to the riverbed before stopping and then paused to look back. There was no pursuit, but they could see Lazuli bunched on the shoulder of the Big Dune.

Over the following weeks, the three remaining pups grew fast. Each day they got up with the rest of the group, sunned and set off foraging. They became more mobile and by the time they were six weeks old seldom lagged behind. Their begging became more and more strident. When an adult they were following found a beetle or a grub, their regular calls would rise to a crescendo. 'Please, pleeease, pleeeeease.'

The pups learned which of the adults of the group were most likely to feed them and which usually ate the food they found themselves. Holly was still lactating and kept most of the food she found during the first hour of foraging. After this, she became more generous and was one of the preferred adults to be with. Their cousins, Risca, Aphrodite and Artemis, were the oldest females apart from their mother and fed them regularly, as did their adolescent sisters and brother from Holly's first litter, Zola, Vialli and Dennis Wise. In contrast, there was little point in following their juvenile sisters, who were still less than six months old. Until recently, they had been dependent on food provided by other group members until the adults began to teach them to forage on their own. They spent most of their time looking for small prey that lived close to the surface like beetles and ants, which they quickly ate themselves. In fact, the juveniles were a positive nuisance for, now that the presence of the new pups had motivated the adults to respond to begging calls, they began to beg again themselves and were sometimes successful in diverting adults into feeding them rather than the pups. They would also grab the food brought to the pups and take it off and eat it. The pups complained loudly – but it was usually too late. More careful helpers, including their mother, Holly, would drop food in front of them and stand guard over them until they had eaten it.

Their brothers and male cousins also fed them regularly, although they were less generous than their sisters. Athos and Porthos were five months old and, like their sisters, gave them food. The juvenile males from Holly's previous litter, like the juvenile females, were a nuisance and competed with them for it.

The pups quickly learned whom it was best to follow: there were twelve group members that fed them regularly but only three pups (after Petal's death), so there was plenty of choice. Adults that were being followed by a begging pup usually gave them the larger prey items that they found. Those that found prey and were not being followed by a begging pup would often kill it, pick it up and run towards the nearest pup. They did not have obvious favourites and were as likely to feed Thumper or Hazel as Flower, though there was a tendency for the female members of the group to feed Flower rather than her brothers.

Though the generosity of the animals varied with their age and sex, there were large differences between individuals. Aphrodite, for example, gave a much higher proportion of her food to the pups than did her sister Risca. In general, the individuals that had often babysat the pups also fed them frequently, while those that had contributed little to babysitting were relatively mean and ate most of their prey themselves.

* * *

Since all group members (apart from the youngest) feed dependent pups, pup feeding provides an ideal opportunity to examine the factors affecting the contribution of different adults to co-operative activities. All group members commonly feed pups relatively little in the first hour of foraging, when they are busy satisfying their own hunger. Then individuals that have foraged successfully start giving more and more of their larger prey to the pups. The extent to which individuals contribute to pup feeding is similar to that for babysitting. Older and heavier animals contribute more than younger and lighter ones and, at any age, females contribute more than males, who spend more time on sentinel duty than females. We looked to see whether brothers and sisters were more generous than cousins or unrelated individuals, but found no sign of this: even male immigrants who are entirely unrelated to the pups feed them as much as other group members.

In naked mole-rats, as well as in many insect societies, some workers specialise in feeding the young, others in guarding them. We examined whether this was the case with meerkat helpers, but there was no evidence that it was. The only exception was a tendency for female helpers to contribute more than males to babysitting and pup-feeding and for males to do more sentinel duty.

We also investigated why some animals consistently contributed to more co-operative activities than others. Who were the super-helpers? They could be of either sex and they were not necessarily the closest relatives of the pups. A first step was to see whether the same animals were generous or mean in successive breeding attempts. Here we got a surprise: differences between individuals were not consistent. Those that had contributed heavily to co-operative activities in one breeding attempt did so less than average in the next. A likely explanation was that generosity led to a decrease in an individual's body condition and this affected their contribution to raising the next litter. To test this, we fed helpers with hardboiled egg at the beginning of the day and found that we could increase the proportion of food that they subsequently gave to pups. When we fed individuals over longer periods, they became super-helpers in consecutive breeding attempts and their tendency to alternate between meanness and generosity disappeared.

While the generosity of helpers was affected by their foraging success and condition, it was also influenced by the behaviour of the pups themselves. When adults are foraging, dependent pups beg continuously, calling around eighty to ninety times per minute, 'wah ... wah ... wah ...' Their rate of calling is related to how hungry they are and can be reduced by feeding them with hardboiled egg. Parents and helpers respond to the begging rate of pups and are more likely to take food to pups that are calling frequently than to those with low calling rates.

Marta Manser recorded groups of pups and made up loops of tape with high and low begging rates. When she used these to supplement the normal begging, the adults increased the proportion of food that they gave to pups and reduced the proportion that they ate themselves. Later, we used the same tapes on helpers with older pups that were able to find food for themselves – and the helpers immediately began to offer food again to the pups despite their age. By collecting blood samples from the animals that had experienced the playbacks, we discovered that pup begging raises the level of cortisol in the blood of helpers, suggesting that cortisol plays a part in controlling helping behaviour.

As the weeks passed and Flower and her two brothers grew larger and stronger, adults brought them larger and more mobile prey. One morning, Aphrodite brought Flower a long, coffin-shaped black beetle. Flower sniffed it hungrily and the beetle spread its pincers in defence. Flower sniffed again – and the beetle snapped its pincers closed on her nose. The pain was blinding and Flower shook her head from side to side, trying to dislodge the beetle. It held on and she went careering through the group shaking her head as she ran. Finally the beetle let go and Flower subsided under a bush. When the adults next brought her one of these beetles, she was careful not to sniff it and bit it hard behind its head before crunching it up.

In the first weeks that the pups foraged with the group, the adults killed or immobilised the prey they brought and removed the stings of scorpions. As the pups grew stronger and more experienced, they gave them more lightly injured prey and, in the end, they gave them prey that was alive and undamaged. Giving pups live prey had the disadvantage for the adults that they had to stand guard over the pup they had just fed – both to prevent the prey from escaping and to make sure that neither the drongos nor the older brothers and sisters stole the prey they had given the pups. Watching the changes in the adults' behaviour, we had the strong impression that they were adapted to teaching the pups how to deal with prey.

But do meerkats really teach pups prey-handling skills? The three criteria that are used to define teaching in animals are that parents should modify their usual behaviour in relation to the stage of development of the young that they are dealing with; that some cost should be involved to the teacher; and that the teacher's behaviour should increase the rate at which the young acquire the relevant skills. No previous studies of mammals had been able to demonstrate that the behaviour of teachers met all three criteria.

The meerkats clearly adjusted the extent to which they disabled prey according to the age of the pups they were feeding. Alex Thornton, a Cambridge graduate student working with the project, recorded the calls of young and old pups. When he played the calls of young pups to groups that were currently feeding older

pups, they increased the extent to which they killed or demo-
bilised prey while, when he played the calls of older pups to
groups feeding young pups, he reduced their tendency to do so.
There is clearly a cost to providing intact prey. Finally, Alex
was able to show that giving pups live prey accelerated their ability
to deal with prey themselves. He fed pups with live or dead
scorpions and subsequently saw how this affected their ability to
handle live scorpions whose sting had been removed. His experi-
ment showed that pups that had been given live scorpions were
better able to cope with live prey than those that had been fed
dead prey, providing conclusive evidence that the meerkats'
behaviour represented a form of teaching.

Sometimes, one of the foraging adults would catch something
and run up to Flower or one of her brothers but, instead of drop-
ping the food in front of them, would eat it themselves, leaving
the pup hungry and frustrated. We called this 'false-feeding' and
similar behaviour has been described in several co-operative birds,
including white-winged choughs. False-feeding is commonly
interpreted as an attempt by helpers to convince other group
members that they are doing more work than is really the case in
order to persuade the adults to allow them to stay in the group.

Is false-feeding really a form of cheating? We were sceptical of
this idea since individuals that false-fed pups make no attempt to
eat the food surreptitiously and breeding females are as likely to
evict super-helpers as other group members. Instead, they appear
to be genuinely undecided as to whether to give away food that
they have found or eat it themselves. We noticed that younger
and lighter meerkats false-fed more than older, heavier ones. And,
when we gave supplementary food to helpers, this reduced the
frequency with which they false-fed pups. In addition, female
helpers (who preferentially feed female pups) are more likely to

false-feed males than females. A more plausible explanation of false-feeding is that individuals that have carried food to pups are affected by signals given off by the pup itself – which may be larger, older or better-fed than the helper had expected. We concluded that false-feeding is unlikely to be a form of cheating.

*   *   *

In the six weeks following their move from the breeding burrow, Whiskers started to use all parts of their range again – from the thorn thickets in the east to the Western Flats below the Big Dune. While Whiskers had been breeding, their neighbours had taken over large parts of their range, which was now seriously dimin-ished. Lazuli had occupied the area around the Big Dune, while to the south, Young Ones had colonised the slopes of the large dunes to the north of the South Flats. Whiskers encountered Young Ones several times on this boundary. In the course of their daily forag-ing trips, Whiskers also met their other neighbours. Compared to Lazuli, which had over thirty members, Whiskers was a small group and, when Whiskers faced them, they would war dance but quickly retreat back to the core of their own range. If Lazuli followed, they would eventually stand their ground. Young Ones and Elveera were smaller and the outcome of encounters was less consistent. Sometimes Whiskers would win and Young Ones would withdraw and sometimes the situation was reversed.

One morning, Whiskers slept in a burrow immediately to the north of the South Flats. They were close to the southern edge of their range but, instead of leading them back north, Holly took the group south into the disputed area. In the morning, they climbed to the dune crest and stood looking across the South Flats to the road and the land beyond. Nothing stirred and there was no sign of Young Ones. Holly led the way down the dune towards a group of thorn trees where there was a large sleeping burrow. The group was bunched and nervous, sniffing at stumps and the bases of trees as they passed. They could smell that other meerkats had been here recently, but Holly went on down the slope.

When they came in sight of the sleeping burrow at the foot of the dune, they stopped. At the mouth of the burrow, there was a single meerkat. Holly watched intently. Beside it, in the burrow entrance, two small faces appeared. It was a Young Ones babysitter with Young Ones pups in the burrow. Hair erect, Holly began a war dance and the rest of the group joined her and streamed down to the burrow. As Whiskers charged, they were hidden from the babysitter, who was caught unawares. Holly flung herself at it and, after a brief spat, the animal ran for its life, leaving Whiskers in possession of the burrow. Holly circled the burrow entrance, sniffed at the burrow walls and then went below ground, followed by Athos and Porthos. The rest of the group poured down behind them, leaving only Risca and the three pups on the surface. After a few minutes they reappeared one by one, shaking sand from their fur. Holly was the last to appear, with blood on her muzzle.

Above ground again, the meerkats engaged in a frenzy of marking. Argon marked the burrow entrance with his anal glands and tore at the vegetation with his teeth. Holly, too, marked the burrow and the base of the clumps of grass. Four of the older group members dug shallow scrapes and defecated. Gradually, the group quietened down and began to forage but Holly was still uneasy. She ceased foraging and led the group north, back up the slope of the dunes where they had come from.

4

ORPHAN

By mid-May, Holly and Aphrodite had ceased to lactate and Flower and her two brothers depended entirely on food brought to them by the other group members. When they were with the group, they still begged regularly but their calls were now louder and deeper. As before, they spent much of their time following one adult after another, though they also kept an eye on other group members and would abandon the adult they were with if another animal seemed to be on the point of capturing something. When it looked as if the adult they were following was about to catch its prey, they gave a loud, bubbling call of excitement.

Throughout the autumn, Whiskers continued to interact with their neighbours, trying to extend the boundaries of their range.

As before, they usually ran from Lazuli and Vivian, while their encounters with Elveera and Young Ones were less predictable. But they did not make much ground, for both Elveera and Young Ones were increasing in size and strength while Whiskers had reared few pups in the last year. With their largest males away visiting other groups in search of mating opportunities for much of the time, they were soon no match for Elveera and Young Ones, let alone Vivian and Lazuli. Gradually, their neighbours began to squeeze them out of their usual hunting grounds, raiding deeper and deeper into their territory. The future of Whiskers looked bleak.

Flower and her brothers grew fast. In smaller meerkat groups where the ratio of pups to helpers is higher, pups get less food although helpers give away a larger proportion of the food they find. Putting together our records for many different groups, we found that pups reared in large groups, where the ratio of helpers to pups was relatively high, consistently received more food and grew faster and were more likely to survive to independence than pups in small ones. However, it was also possible that some groups had more productive territories than others and that pups raised in these groups grew well and showed higher survival, so that the number of helpers was relatively high. To be sure that the number of helpers in the group affected pup growth directly, we temporarily increased the ratio of helpers to pups by removing pups for a couple of hours. When we reduced the number of pups in the group, the amount of food received by each of the remaining pups increased and they gained more weight. In addition, helpers gave away a smaller proportion of the food they found and so they, too, gained more weight. We also tried introducing pups of the same age from one group to another and found that helpers fed them quite readily and that increases in pup numbers reduced the weight gain of pups and helpers. Relatively high ratios of helpers to pups are good for everyone – another benefit of increased group size.

With many animals, differences in the age and condition of mothers have important consequences for the development and survival of their offspring. For example, the rate at which red deer grow in the first months of life is affected by characteristics of their mothers – including age, size, condition and social rank. For meerkats, the mother's characteristics are less important to pups than the size of the groups they are brought up in. The effects of differences in early growth persist throughout their lifespans. Light pups are less effective at foraging as adolescents. As they develop into yearlings, pups born in small groups have the additional disadvantage that they have to give away a larger proportion of the food they find to rear the next litter of pups, with the result that they grow more slowly than those in larger groups.

By the end of June, Thumper and Hazel had grown into healthy juveniles. Flower was no smaller than her brothers and was at least as aggressive as they were. Male and female meerkat pups – unlike red deer – are the same weight at birth and have similar growth rates. The absence of any sex differences in birth weight and early growth reflects the lack of a marked difference in body size between male and female adults which, in turn, is related to their monogamous mating system. In most polygynous mammals, where males are substantially larger than females, males have higher average birth weights and faster growth rates.

* * *

Midwinter in the Kalahari is in late July. The days are bright and cool and the meerkats continue to forage throughout the day. By early August, Flower and her brothers were over three months old and were active, playful juveniles. They now spent most of their time digging for food themselves rather than following foraging adults. When they did pursue adults and beg for food, they were often ignored. They were still relatively ineffective foragers themselves and seldom dug deep holes for the larger prey, like scorpions and geckos. Instead, they fed on the small beetles that lived around the base of the grass tufts or on ants that lived just below the surface.

Flower gradually picked up the skills necessary to survive. When the adults found ants' nests, they broke them open and quickly licked up all the available larvae and workers before the soldiers streamed up. Then they would beat a hasty retreat to avoid being bitten. When the pups first began feeding on their own, they enthusiastically investigated sites that adults had left. The soldier ants would attack them and the pups would career through the group, trying to wipe them off. Flower quickly discovered that disturbed ants seldom provide an easy meal and it was better to find her own ants' nests. She also learned how to deal with the other prey that the adults brought to her. She found out that the black bombardier beetles, with delicate white edging on their wing cases, were good to eat but, given a chance, squirted burning juices on their faces. She discovered that the large black millipedes that shared the meerkats' burrows with them exuded a foul-smelling juice but were perfectly edible, if they were first rolled across the sand to wipe off their secretions.

Sub-adults and yearlings often steal food that has been given to pups, and Flower learned to protect the food that she had been given from her older sisters and brothers. When she received bigger items she could not eat all at once, like larger scorpions or geckos, she hunched over them and retreated, growling, into the clefts at the base of a bush where she could not be attacked from behind. The meerkats often found long, pink burrowing skinks, much like slow worms. They usually ate them tail first, chewing their way down the body as the worm writhed and turned. This took a while and often attracted the attention of the older adolescents, who would grab the other end of the worm, so a tug of war followed.

Flower and her brothers sometimes still begged from adults that were digging holes, climbing into the hole ahead of the digging adult to try to get to the food. The adults responded by blocking access to the holes and growling at the juveniles. When the adults found large millipedes, they would normally roll them in the sand and then bite them in half, pulling the soft entrails out of the rear end before eating them greedily. The pups would do their best to grab the other half and the discovery of these large millipedes often led to repeated battles between adults and juveniles. In the middle of the battle, the front end of the millipede sometimes walked away while the meerkats were still fighting over its rear end.

Flower came to recognise danger from the responses of other group members. She watched the reactions of guards to different birds and became adept at distinguishing between those that were dangerous and those that were not. She could quickly tell the difference between the hornbills that flapped between trees and presented no risk and the pale chanting goshawks that eyed them from the tree tops and would attack pups if given an opportunity. She learned to tell the difference between the large, slow-circling vultures and the faster flying eagles that were dangerous predators. Above all, she soon recognised the black head, black underwings and white belly of the martial eagle, the meerkats' main enemy.

Though Flower and her brothers did not yet act as sentinels

themselves, they learned the significance of the different alarm calls given by the adults. They no longer ran to the nearest adult when they heard an alarm call. Instead, they looked up when they heard the call given for an aerial danger, looked around when they heard the call for terrestrial predators, and looked at the ground when they heard the growls and spitting calls for snakes. They also learned to pelt for the nearest bolthole when sentinels gave an urgent alarm call.

When the group encountered small snakes, they commonly attacked them and occasionally ate them. In contrast, when they came across the enormous, rough-scaled puff adders or hooded, rust-red Cape cobras they formed a half-circle around them and mobbed them, growling and giving spitting alarm calls. The Cape cobra is the most dangerous of all the Kalahari's snakes, fast and aggressive, with a neurotoxic poison that can be fatal to other animals, including meerkats. Animals in the front rank lunged towards the snake, which sometimes struck at them, but they were usually careful to keep out of its range.

Many mongooses are resistant to the cytotoxic venom of vipers and adders as well as to the neurotoxic venoms of cobras and related snakes, though the resistance of meerkats has yet to be studied. However, severe bites can still be lethal to meerkats as well as to many much larger mammals. Mobbing large and dangerous snakes is risky and it was not clear what the meerkats achieved by it. Beke Graw, a student from Zurich, made a detailed study of mobbing. Her work showed that the meerkats mobbed cobras, the most dangerous of the snakes, more frequently and for longer than the slower-moving puff adders or harmless mole-snakes. Juveniles spent less time mobbing than yearlings and did not adjust their behaviour to the degree of risk posed by the prey to the same extent. Older animals were also less likely to mob snakes for long periods than yearlings or two-year-olds and males mobbed for longer than females, especially when pups were present in the group.

Individuals may benefit from mobbing in several ways. First, it alerts all group members to the presence of cryptic predators, making sure that they do not put themselves at risk unknowingly. Second, it provides younger animals with important experience of the responses of predators, under circumstances where they can control the distance between themselves and the animal they are mobbing. And, third, it may encourage cryptic predators to leave the area. For example, leopards that are being mobbed by jackals are unlikely to be able to hunt successfully and will move on to other hunting grounds, reducing the immediate risk that they will not be noticed and will, later on, be in a position to launch a dangerous attack. Similarly, most snakes mobbed by meerkats commonly move away once the animals allow them to go, though puff adders generally remain where they are until the animals lose interest.

Since even midday temperatures were now low, there was no need for the meerkats to rest in the shade. The animals foraged throughout the day until it was time to head for their sleeping burrow. Food was scarcer and many of their larger prey were inactive, deep underground. They spent more time scratching on the surface for small beetles and ants, and lost weight. By mid-afternoon, they often started to head for their sleeping burrow and would group around the entrance, sunning or grooming each other, before disappearing one by one.

Whiskers continued to push out the boundary of their range but their relationships with their neighbours remained unchanged. When they encountered Lazuli or Vivian, they beat a hasty retreat until they were deep inside their territory. The outcome of encounters with Young Ones and Elveera was less certain and either one might chase away the others. At the end of August, Whiskers once again visited the South Flats and this time met Young Ones on the slopes of the dunes above their sleeping burrows. They attacked and, after a mêlée, Young Ones turned and ran. Young Ones contained an unusually large number of females and some of them must have been of interest for, a day later, the four Whiskers adult males, Beetle, Delpheus, Lancelot and Athos, left the group to follow Young Ones at a distance. Over the next month the same group of males regularly went visiting neighbouring groups on the lookout for willing females.

*   *   *

By the beginning of September, the coldest days were past but the desert was still dry and dead. When the wind was in the west, it drove in banks of high cloud – but there was no rain. Eventually the first rain fell in short, sharp showers followed by a heavy downpour the next day. Within a few days, the ground was covered with the broad green leaves of desert lilies, which produced large, many-headed flowers. The camel thorn trees broke out in green leaf, mixed with yellow flowers.

Rain is the lifeblood of the desert. The smell of rain in the desert is the smell of plants growing, of animals breeding, of life stirring. After long periods without rain, green vegetation disappears and all forms of life shrivel and lose their colour. Then it rains and life is quickly renewed. The trees are full of courting doves, pygmy falcons display from the top of the camel thorns and, one by one, the dominant female meerkats swell with their next litters. The sourgrass grows, sometimes to waist height so that the dune slacks look like fields of winter wheat. Then it's hard to remember that this is a desert.

Sometimes, in the course of their travels, the meerkats came across yellow mongooses, which share their ranges with them. These are similar in size to meerkats but are better at catching fast-moving prey like lizards and spend more time feeding on vertebrates than meerkats. Since a group of mongooses foraging together would disturb alert, mobile prey, they forage on their own or in pairs. However, several individuals often share a sleeping burrow and, as in meerkats, subordinates help to feed pups produced by dominant breeders. To minimise the risk of predation while they are out foraging, yellow mongooses usually keep to areas where there is plentiful ground cover and also forage later into the evening when eagles are no longer active. When the meerkats met yellow mongooses above ground, the two species usually ignored or avoided each other but when the meerkats came across them in a burrow or bolthole, they growled and displayed at the burrow entrance. The most northerly populations of meerkats also share their ranges with groups of dwarf mongooses. Like meerkats, these feed mostly on insects and less mobile vertebrates so they can forage in closely-knit groups without disturbing the animals they are hunting.

*   *   *

By late September, Holly was pregnant with the first litter of the new season. When she stood up to sun, the curve of her belly was clearly visible and when she walked there was a bulge on either side of her flanks. As the pups grew inside her, she became more and more aggressive. She was particularly intolerant of her three nieces, Risca, who was now two, Artemis and Aphrodite, who were still yearlings. All three of them had also conceived and were visibly pregnant.

At some times Holly would go up to the females while they were feeding and displace them from the hole they were digging with furious growls. At others, she would suddenly turn on them and attack them. They hunched up, protecting their faces while Holly bit them repeatedly at the base of their tail. When they walked, she sometimes slammed them sideways with a twist of her hips. Her nieces made no attempt to retaliate and instead did their best to placate her, rushing up to her and chattering anxiously. Holly would knock them aside and move on. In the evening, the other females often tried to groom her. Sometimes Holly would allow this and lie back contentedly, but as the birth of her pups approached, she became more and more intolerant and brusquely rejected their advances.

Finally, Holly's tolerance snapped. One morning, as the group spread out to forage, she attacked Risca, who ran away with Holly in hot pursuit. Holly chased her for two hundred yards and then lost interest, walking back to the others while Risca sat and watched her. When they moved on, Risca followed at a distance. After Risca had left, Holly's aggression focused on her other two nieces, Artemis and Aphrodite. Eventually, Holly attacked each of them in turn and chased them out of the group. Risca came to join them and the trio watched the main party anxiously as they moved off. That night, as Whiskers relaxed at their sleeping burrow, the three females tried to sneak back in but Holly saw them and again chased them away. They slept in a bolthole half a mile from the main burrow, huddling together against the cold.

Next morning, the three evicted females tried again to rejoin Whiskers, but again Holly saw them. This time, instead of a direct chase, she started to war dance at them, rocking to and fro between her front and hind legs, her tail straight up and her hair erect. The others joined her and soon the entire group was war dancing at the three outcasts. Suddenly, Holly charged and the three females ran for their lives. When the group set off on their daily journey the three were out of sight.

In the days after the eviction of the three females, Holly continued to swell. Her belly was now close to its limit and she walked uncomfortably with a rolling gait. One night, she went down to sleep swollen – and emerged the next morning slim and svelte, with blood on her vulva. The group sunned and began to forage around the burrow and Risca appeared on the edge of the group. She was thin and clearly no longer pregnant. Holly made no move to chase her away and she rejoined the group without mishap. When Holly and the rest moved away to forage, Risca stayed behind and babysat the pups. By the evening, the pups' begging and their attempts to suckle had stimulated Risca to lactate and there were wet marks around her nipples. Over the next week, the group set out each day on its daily foraging trek and the older helpers took turns at babysitting at the breeding burrow in the dunes. Sometimes it was Risca, sometimes one of the yearlings, Vialli or Zola or sometimes one of the males. Flower and her brothers were still too young to babysit and went with the others each day.

Ten days after Holly had given birth, the group set out from their sleeping burrow in the eastern plateau. They were in an area of broken dunes and visibility was poor. It was windy and the meerkats were nervous. Leading them, Holly came to the crest of a dune and waited to give the others time to catch up. Suddenly there was a rush of air and she was fifty feet up in the claws of a martial eagle that had come fast and silently along the face of the dune. Huge talons punctured her lungs and the eagle carried her off to the shade of a shepherd's tree to feed.

The rest of the group realised the danger immediately and ran back to the nearest burrow, where they gathered at the entrance.

They were quickly aware of Holly's absence and were nervous and disoriented. Argon ran from individual to individual making 'lost' calls, clearly looking for her. Gradually, they relaxed and spread out to feed – but they were still jumpy and reacted strongly to the alarm calls of the accompanying drongos. In the early afternoon, they returned to the breeding burrow where Risca was babysitting.

After Holly's death Risca continued to suckle the orphaned pups. She was now the oldest female by several months and established her dominance over Holly's daughters, Zola and Vialli, and the other females without difficulty. Three days after Holly's death, Aphrodite and Artemis rejoined the group and submitted to Risca. Artemis was still pregnant but, like Risca, Aphrodite had lost her pups while she was away from the group, and she joined Risca in suckling Holly's pups. At the end of the month, Artemis produced one male pup, which was subsequently killed by a predator. At around the same time, Artemis' daughter, Ugly, was badly savaged in a fight between Whiskers and Young Ones, but lived on.

* * *

When breeding female meerkats die, all females over a year old compete intensively for the breeding role. Individuals that, the day before, had been living peaceably with each other, rarely showing any sign of aggression, suddenly turn into vicious rivals. Sometimes – as in the case of Risca – the situation is rapidly settled, the violence subsides and the other females resume their usual behaviour, but, especially if two or more females are closely matched in age and weight, it can last several months, only ending when one competitor is either killed or chased out of the group. When subordinate female meerkats compete for the dominant position, it is almost always the oldest female in the group that succeeds, though if there are several females from the same or successive litters, this rule is sometimes broken and then it is generally the heaviest of the competitors that becomes dominant.

Newly dominant female meerkats show increased levels of oestrogen and testosterone. The frequency with which they threaten or attack other group members rises, as does their marking of burrows or stumps with their anal glands. They also increase in body size and weight and establish their dominance over all other group members, including the males. Females that have competed with them resume their role as subordinates and often play an important part in rearing their pups. The death of dominant females is followed by similar events in several other co-operative mammals. For example, in naked mole-rats, the death or removal of dominant females leads to a period of intense competition between subordinates until one female establishes dominance. Over the course of the next year, newly dominant females kill or evict all the females that have competed with them.

The accession of Risca to the breeding role placed the dominant male, Argon, in a dilemma. Risca and all the other females in the group were his daughters and rejected any sexual advances he made. He now joined the other males in visiting other groups, looking for breeding opportunities, spending less and less time in Whiskers. On many days, the adult males would sidle away soon after the group had stopped sunning and would only return in the evening, looking tired and smelling of other groups. Between the ages of one and three years, most subordinate male meerkats spend an increasing proportion of their time prospecting for mating opportunities in neighbouring groups, initially staying away for less than a day, but sometimes going away for several days at a time. Eventually, they all leave their natal group permanently. Both Argon and Delpheus finally left Whiskers and disappeared from the study area. After they had gone, there was no immigrant male left, though Beetle established himself as dominant to the other males. Whiskers began to attract roving males from elsewhere and there was commonly at least one other male lurking on its periphery.

*   *   *

Females refuse to breed with their fathers or brothers in many birds and mammals living in stable social groups. The likely reason is that close relatives have an increased chance of carrying the same rare, deleterious recessive genes that are likely to affect the survival of offspring that inherit them from both parents. Though not many studies have been able to compare the survival of offspring born of matings between close relatives with those between unrelated individuals, almost all have shown that close inbreeding depresses their survival. These effects can be substantial. For example, estimates for humans suggest that as many as forty-two per cent of babies born to parent-offspring or brother-sister mating might be expected to die before or soon after birth, twenty-four per cent of those born to matings between half-siblings and thirteen per cent of those born to matings between full cousins.

In animals that live in stable groups, females have evolved several ways of avoiding inbreeding. In species where the tenure of dominant males is long so that a male's daughter commonly matures while he is still the dominant breeding male in their group, females commonly disperse to breed with unrelated males elsewhere. For example, in the groups of pied babblers that occupy territories along the riverbed, dominant males can hold their position for five or more years while their daughters are ready to breed in their second year; females usually disperse soon after reaching adolescence. Where the turnover of dominant males is more rapid, females commonly remain in their original group. If their father is still in the group, they often delay the onset of sexual maturity. For example, experiments with deer mice in North America show that females do this if their father is present in the group. In meerkats, subordinate females seldom attempt to breed unless there is an unrelated male in their group or their group is visited by unrelated rovers from other groups. Similar mechanisms may occur in humans: several recent studies have found that girls raised in nuclear families whose father is present reach puberty later than those whose father is absent or has been replaced by an unrelated male.

When female mammals remain in the group where they were born, they commonly refuse mating attempts by their brothers. In some species, they appear to recognise close kin, while in others, they avoid mating with males born in the group or males that were already in the group when they were born. In several human societies, too, females rarely breed with individuals familiar since childhood. However, recognition and avoidance of breeding with close relatives is not universal, and, where individuals of both sexes commonly disperse into surrounding populations and the probability that close relatives will breed with each other is low, females will often breed with their brothers if they happen to encounter them.

Despite the disadvantages of breeding with close relatives, there are a small number of species where breeding with close relatives is the norm. One of these is the naked mole-rat; both sexes commonly remain in the colony where they are born and breed with other individuals born in the same group. Presumably, the costs of dispersal to female mole-rats are so high that they outweigh those of breeding with related males. In addition, once a population adopts a practice of inbreeding, deleterious recessive genes are commonly expressed, their carriers are eliminated and their frequency in the population drops, as do the disadvantages of inbreeding. For example, when animal populations are reduced to such low levels that inbreeding between close relatives is inevitable, deleterious recessive genes are purged from the population and further inbreeding no longer depresses the growth and survival of offspring. However, the lack of genetic diversity may have other disadvantages.

* * *

After Risca had assumed the dominant position, life returned to normal for Flower and her brothers. The group would leave at dawn to forage, rest during the heat of the day, forage again in the afternoon and then either return to the previous night's burrow or sleep at one of the other burrows in their range. In October, Risca came into season and mated with one of the roving males that regularly tailed the group. She was less assertive than Holly and her capacity to control the other females was weak. All the six females over a year old mated with males from other groups and also became pregnant. Even Artemis, who still had two small pups from her last litter, mated again and started to swell. In the morning, the seven females stood in line, exposing their bulging stomachs to the sun. In the latter half of their gestation period, they became more aggressive and the spats between them more frequent and intense.

In the month that followed, all the females gave birth in turn. Pregnant female meerkats – both dominants and subordinates – commonly kill any pups born in the group, and, soon after each litter was born, the pups were killed by one of the other pregnant females. Risca was the first to give birth. In the evening, she went down to the sleeping burrow heavily pregnant and next morning emerged deflated. Aphrodite, her cousin, who was still pregnant, came after her from the burrow with blood on her face and chest, having gained a suspicious amount of weight overnight. When the group left to forage no babysitters remained behind, indicating that there were no pups left alive in the burrow.

Zola and Vialli, Holly's eldest daughters, were the next to give birth, two days apart. This time their pups were killed by Artemis. Two weeks later, Aphrodite, Aramis and Wahine produced their litters. All of them were again killed by Artemis, the last pregnant female. Finally, three days later, Artemis produced a litter of three. There were now no other pregnant females in the group and her litter survived.

Infanticide by females is frequent in many mammals and usually occurs in the first few days of life of a new litter. Dominant females commonly kill pups born to their subordinate daughters – but if subordinate females are pregnant, they will also kill their mother's pups or each other's and there is no indication that females are less likely to kill pups born to close relatives than those born to more distantly related females. In almost all cases, the killer is pregnant: subordinate females rarely kill pups if they are not pregnant and even dominant females commonly spare litters born to subordinates at times when they are not pregnant. Since pregnant females show increased levels of circulating testosterone in their blood and are obviously aggressive, it seems likely that infanticidal tendencies are controlled by sex hormones, as they are in male rodents.

Meerkats benefit from increases in group size – so why do females kill each other's newborn young? The close association between pregnancy and infanticide suggests that females who will shortly give birth kill other females' pups to protect their own litter from competition. Where the ratio of pups to helpers is relatively high, pups receive less food, grow more slowly and are less likely to survive. There is another reason why older pups threaten litters born soon after them. Where two litters are born at the same time, the movements of the group are timed to coincide with the needs of the oldest litter. As soon as the oldest litter of pups is ready to travel, the helpers encourage them to come on the day's march – which then usually ends up at another sleeping burrow. Younger pups consequently either have to begin to travel with the group at a relatively young age – or are likely to be deserted at the breeding burrow, where they will certainly die. However, if they do leave with the group, they are commonly unable to keep up and are eventually abandoned. Finally, infanticide is an effective way of getting a wet-nurse. Females whose pups have recently been killed are hormonally primed to lactate to their own litter and commonly respond to pups subsequently born to other females by suckling them. If a pregnant female kills other females' pups, it is more likely that they will lactate to her own litter, increasing the milk available to her own pups, raising their growth rate and improving their chances of survival.

* * *

For the first month after the birth of Artemis' pups, the meerkats left a babysitter at the burrow each day to guard them against marauders or predators. Artemis herself needed to forage to replenish her milk and Risca, as the dominant female, played no part. Each day when the group began to leave the breeding burrow to forage, one of the adults would hang back and babysit the pups. On some days it was one of the adult females, on others one of the adult males. Since their own pups had been killed, Aphrodite, Zola, Vialli, Aramis and Wahine were all primed to lactate and suckled Artemis' pups regularly, emerging in the morning with wet circles round their nipples.

By the end of their first month, Artemis' pups were ready to travel with the rest of the group and the Whiskers left the breeding burrow beside the big camel thorn tree. Aphrodite and Vialli first coaxed and then gently shepherded them away and, once they had left, their only option was to follow the group. Flower and the others guarded them carefully and sometimes carried them in their mouths when they got left behind. That night they slept at a new burrow and, the next morning, the pups followed the adults readily when the group went on their daily trip.

When the pups were foraging with the group, they begged continuously for food. One or other of them often followed Flower, calling incessantly while she dug for prey. The hungrier the pups were, the more they called and Flower found that she could quieten them by giving them a beetle or a grub. If she then moved off quickly, the pups would stay behind and she would be free to forage without disturbance for a while. After she had satisfied her own hunger, she gave more of the large prey items she found to the pups. Sometimes, she would dig up a grub or a barking gecko and run back to the foraging pups to feed one or other of them. Occasionally, they were obviously sated although they continued to call and then Flower would eat the prey herself. Thumper and Hazel helped to feed the pups too, but they were less generous than Flower and the pups did not follow them so readily.

5

BROTHERS IN ARMS

Flower, Thumper and Hazel were now well-grown yearlings. They were skilful foragers, often digging deep holes for larger prey. Flower could identify the burrows of scorpions and knew how to tunnel down almost vertically to get to them. She had discovered that, when she was digging out barking geckos, they commonly ran out of the side tunnel of their main burrow and lay perfectly still on the surface of the sand. So she interrupted her digging at regular intervals to check that her quarry had not escaped. She now knew to investigate the shallower burrows of striped mice in case they contained pups and that it was worth investigating the holes where tortoises had laid their eggs. Most important of all, she had learned when to abandon a dig in order to avoid spending time and effort on unnecessary digging. The yearlings also learned which of the other animals that moved through their territory constituted a risk. They kept away from the feet of the eland and gemsbok when they came across them but otherwise paid them little attention. Sometimes, they encountered tortoises on their daily foraging trips and, at first, had not known what to make of them and sniffed all around their shells, nipping at their armpits and faces. They quickly learned that they were too well armoured to be potential meals and soon they disregarded them too. From the reactions of the other group members, they had learned to be alarmed by the scent of wildcats and jackals – but not by the smell of porcupines or aardvarks.

After sunning in the morning, or when the group rested at midday, Flower and her brothers often played together, chasing each other round bushes, ambushing their partners, wrestling and mock-fighting. Play is energetic and hungry animals do not play much. By provisioning some juveniles with hard boiled eggs, Lynda Sharpe was able to show that increased food availability caused a rapid increase in the amount of time individuals spent playing. Play usually incorporates elements of adult behaviour – attack, defence, aggression, stalking and mating – and probably helps individuals to develop the motor skills that they will use later in life, though other functions have been suggested. Perhaps play allows animals to improve their fighting behaviour or to establish dominance relationships or to develop close social bonds that may be useful when they are driven out of their original group. By following individual meerkats throughout their development, Lynda investigated whether individuals that played a lot as juveniles or subadults were better fighters as adults or whether they were more likely to disperse together. They weren't, and her study provided no evidence that the amount individuals played influenced their social relationships.

Flower and her two brothers now played an important part in group activities. When she had satisfied her immediate hunger in the morning, she was often one of the first to go on guard. Sometimes there were convenient dead trees where it was possible to find a secure seat some feet above ground. More commonly, there was only a drie doring bush where she had to balance herself, swaying precariously, three or four feet above ground level. When she was settled on her perch, she began to give regular low-pitched calls which told the other members of her family that she was on lookout and that they could forage safely. While she was on guard, the group searched for food, moving steadily on, and, after three or four minutes, she was left behind and climbed clumsily down and ran after her retreating group. This was always a dangerous time, as she might have to run several hundred yards without the protection of the others. Once she had rejoined the rest, Flower began to forage again. After she had satisfied her hunger once more – and particularly if she had caught and eaten some particularly large prey – she might take another turn at guard duty.

As summer turned into autumn, the days shortened, the grass died back and the camel thorns lost their leaves. Risca had been attacking Aphrodite and Artemis with increasing frequency. They grovelled to her and tried to groom her, but she became more and more intolerant of their presence. When they hunched up to protect themselves, she bit them repeatedly at the base of the tail, in just the same way that Holly had done to her. One day she chased Aphrodite and Artemis out of the group. They spent several days hanging around and were chased away repeatedly by Risca and then disappeared from the study area. We never discovered their fate.

Dispersing females virtually never join established breeding groups, but they often take up with wandering bands of males and can form new breeding groups. Sometimes, they move considerable distances and we occasionally hear of parties of unusually tame meerkats turning up thirty or more kilometres away. However, the whole area is saturated with meerkat territories and splinter groups that attempt to settle are commonly attacked and driven out by established groups. Even when dispersing females found a new group, the most dominant individual usually evicts other founding females within a year. Forced to travel through unfamiliar country and to sleep in shallow boltholes where they can easily be dug out by jackals or honey badgers, most dispersing meerkats are probably killed by predators within a year of leaving their original group unless they manage to establish themselves as dominant breeders in new groups.

*   *   *

Understanding the strategies used by dominant females to monopolise reproduction is the key to understanding meerkat society. Through regular aggression, dominant females are usually able to prevent others from attaining breeding condition and conceiving. Subordinate females show lower levels of oestrogen than dominants, but if the dominant female dies or is removed, the oestrogen levels of subordinates rise and they rapidly conceive.

Zoologists disagree over the way in which dominant females influence the hormonal status and fertility of subordinates. One possibility is that dominants constrain the fertility of subordinates directly through aggression aimed at those that show signs of entering breeding condition, which may reduce their level of sex hormones. Another is that dominants usually ensure that subordinates' attempts to reproduce are futile by killing their pups, encouraging them to abstain from breeding. And a third suggestion is that subordinates rarely breed because they often lack access to unrelated males. Both constraint and restraint seem likely to be involved. The immediate effects of the removal of dominants on the hormonal status and behaviour of subordinates strongly suggest that some form of direct constraint is involved – while evidence that the probability that subordinates will attempt to breed is affected by their weight as well as by their access to unrelated males argues for some form of reproductive restraint by subordinates.

Another way in which dominant females monopolise reproduction is by the eviction of other females. If you look at the age structure of meerkat groups, a striking fact hits you. While dominant females are often six, eight or even ten years old, there are virtually no subordinate females over three years old and relatively few over two. Since subordinate females (unlike subordinate males) almost never leave groups voluntarily, this means that virtually all of them are evicted before they are three. The likely reason for this is that the dominant female's capacity to prevent subordinate females from breeding declines as the subordinates get older, stronger and more experienced. If they cannot prevent them conceiving, the chance that there will be a pregnant female in the group when they bear pups will be high. Moreover, older, larger and stronger females are more likely to challenge dominants for their position and to win if they do so. It makes sense to evict them before losing control.

Sometimes, yearling females are driven out, too, especially if they are pregnant; this is probably a sensible precaution given that pregnant females regularly kill pups born to other females. Solitary living is acutely dangerous for meerkats and is extremely stressful. Females living outside the group show substantial increases in levels of cortisol and if they are pregnant they usually abort their litters. After dominant females have given birth, they often allow previously evicted females back into the group and these animals can play an important role in helping to rear their young. Cortisol levels are related to the extent to which individuals help to feed pups, so the eviction of younger subordinates may encourage them to be generous helpers.

* * *

The older Whiskers males had taken to leaving the group soon after they started to forage and to hang around neighbouring groups in the hope of mating with subordinate females. Led by Lancelot, Athos, Dennis and Beetle, they would visit Elveera, Young Ones or even Lazuli, looking for opportunities to mate. They sometimes stayed away from Whiskers overnight and Hazel and Thumper began to go with them. When the males were away roving, Whiskers was depleted and became even less likely to win encounters with its neighbours.

Eventually, the Whiskers males went roving once too often. In mid-June, all ten of them, including Hazel and Thumper, left the group to investigate their neighbours. Vivian, whose range was to the east, had grown over the last twelve months and now contained twelve males over a year old. Like the Whiskers males, most of them were brothers and they were all closely related to the adult females in their community and so had no breeding opportunities at home. They, too, spent much of their time visiting groups whose ranges adjoined their own. Recently, they had started to go further afield and by late June, had begun to hang around Whiskers.

One day, after all the Whiskers males had slipped away to visit

Young Ones, a coalition of eight Vivian males arrived at Whiskers. They were all sons of the dominant female but several of them came from different litters. The oldest was a large male called Basil, who was four years old, followed by Izit, a slightly smaller male from a different litter who was six months younger. Though he was younger, Izit was dominant to Basil and to the other males in the group. These included two brothers from a subsequent litter, Zaphod and Yossarian, who were two and a half, and three from Vivian's next litter, Genghis, Attila and Alexander, who were just over two years old. It was a powerful alliance of large animals.

The Vivian males reached Whiskers midway through the morning while they were looking for food. Risca saw them and stared at them, but they kept their distance and she returned to foraging. Finally, Izit saw an opportunity. Wahine was feeding at the edge of the group and was partly isolated. Tail down, he scuttled from bush to bush until he was within a few yards of her – and then ran forward and sniffed her. She turned and stood her ground and he immediately tried to mate but she refused. Izit was in the open and susceptible to attack and was poised to run. But nothing happened. No resident males came bounding towards him. He could see females all round as well as some juveniles, but no males. He relaxed and began to follow Wahine.

Izit was rapidly joined by the rest of his brothers. Over the course of the day, the Vivian males explored the group, sniffing and courting the older females, several of whom mated readily with them. In the late afternoon, Lancelot and Dennis Wise returned from a visit to Lazuli. When they tried to re-enter the group, they were immediately attacked and driven away by Basil and Izit. An hour later, Athos and Beetle showed up with Hazel and Thumper in tow. They received the same treatment and were forced to go and sleep at boltholes close by. Next day, the Whiskers males left to try their luck at other groups and made no further attempts to rejoin Whiskers. It was the last occasion on which Flower saw Hazel and Thumper.

The Vivian males quickly established themselves as residents of Whiskers. The new males were unrelated to Risca, who mated readily with several of them. The other group members soon came to tolerate them and the daily activity cycle continued unchanged. As soon as they had established themselves, the Vivian males began to compete for the dominant position. Since Izit had been the most dominant of the brothers before they left their original group, he now asserted his status in Whiskers, marking frequently and threatening his brothers if they approached Risca. Faced with this situation, his older brother, Basil, left Whiskers and returned to Vivian, subsequently teaming up with a younger brother. Three other males from Vivian joined their brothers in Whiskers, bringing the total number of immigrants to ten.

Though Izit initially established himself as dominant in Whiskers, there were several other immigrant males in the group, all of whom were unrelated to the females and so could assume the top position. His younger brothers, Zaphod, Yossarian, Alexander and Zazu, one of the most recent immigrants, challenged him in rapid succession. Exhausted, he was eventually defeated and subsequently bullied by the other males.

While the Vivian males were well established in Whiskers, they were used to spending much of their time roving and continued to do so. Soon after defeating Izit, they all went off on an extended trip to inspect the neighbouring groups. Zazu was the first back and immediately took control in Whiskers on his return. But his reign was brief, for his brothers came back one by one and three weeks later he was deposed.

The four younger males, Zaphod, Yossarian, Genghis and

Alexander, now fought for dominance. Yossarian and Zaphod were older by three months and much larger than Ghenghis and Alexander. Zaphod and Yossarian were closely matched, so there was no quick outcome. Towards the end of September, Zaphod emerged as the most dominant of the brothers and began to establish his position, mark regularly and restrict his brothers' access to Risca. Over the next few months, his brothers regularly went roving and several of them left the group.

The immigration of a group of males as large as that of Basil, Izit and their brothers is not common in meerkats. After the death of a dominant male, any immigrant male already resident in the group usually takes over. This is probably why males that have moved into the group with one older brother often remain as subordinates. However, where many males have immigrated together, the younger and more subordinate males generally continue to rove and eventually leave. Presumably, the potential benefits of roving exceed those of waiting at the end of a long queue for the dominant position. Very occasionally, resident dominant males are displaced by groups of roving males. Events of this kind are only likely to occur where breeding groups have grown large enough to generate sizeable splinter groups of rovers capable of overcoming the defences of resident immigrant males and their sons and driving them out. They are rare in meerkats, though they occur regularly in some other social mammals, including langurs and lions.

When a dominant male dies or leaves and there is no resident immigrant male in the group, roving males from other groups show increasing interest, probably reacting to olfactory cues from the dominant female. Initially, they are chased away by males born in the group, but eventually they come to be tolerated and one or two take up residence and rapidly establish themselves as dominants. However, where the group is large and there are many home-born males that have not yet dispersed, immigrants are often prevented from joining and, sometimes, there is no immigrant male for up to a year or more. Even then, dominant females very rarely mate with males born in the same group. Instead, they usually mate with roving males that visit the group, before their sons chase them away. However, where population density is low and rovers are scarce, dominant females sometimes cease to breed – in some cases, for a full season.

*   *   *

When you observe animals of a species new to you, you are sometimes struck by novel things that you have not seen before. When I first started watching meerkats, I was fascinated by the regular rota of sentinels, for none of the other animals I had observed had ever done anything like this. In other cases, you are surprised at the things they do not do which are common in other species. In meerkats one of these surprises is the failure of immigrant males to kill dependent pups.

In 1961, a Japanese primatologist, Yukimaru Sugiyama, watched as a band of seven male gray langurs expelled the resident dominant male from a breeding group in South India. Like meerkats, langurs live in stable groups of ten to thirty, with a single dominant breeding male in each group. Unlike meerkats, males that emigrate from their natal group usually join bachelor groups that commonly invade breeding groups and evict resident males. In the days after the takeover, the new males in Sugiyama's group fought among themselves until only one was left. The new dominant male then bit and killed all the six infants in the group. Soon afterwards, there was an increase in sexual activity among females. Subsequent observations at other sites showed that takeovers by males were relatively frequent and were commonly associated with infant deaths.

The violence associated with takeovers was surprising, for previous studies of gray langurs had stressed the peaceable and relaxed nature of social relationships between adult males and had contrasted this with the behaviour of baboons and macaques. Sugiyama argued that males might kill infants to avoid the delay in female receptivity that occurred when females were rearing their offspring. A common response to his argument was that infanticide must be a pathological consequence of high local population density, but subsequent studies of langurs by Sarah Hrdy from Harvard showed that male infanticide often occured when new males took over a group and that females whose infants had been killed became sexually receptive within a few days and copulated with the new dominant male.

The average tenure of dominant males in langur groups is very short – commonly no more than eighteen months – while females that have produced an infant often do not conceive again for up to a year. As a result, killing dependent juveniles increases the number of females an incoming male can mate with during his period of tenure. The juveniles are, after all, likely to be unrelated to him, so there is little disadvantage. More clearly than any other example, male infanticide crystallises the contrast between explanations of social behaviour that rely on benefits to groups, populations or species and explanations that rely only on benefits to individuals. Infant-killing by incoming males reduces the breeding success of females and the potential growth rate both of the group and of the population – but persists because it increases the breeding success of individual males.

In the years following the discovery of regular infanticide by male langurs, studies of other monkeys, social carnivores (including lions) and social rodents confirmed that immigrant males commonly kill dependent young. But not meerkats. Although infanticide by females is common, we have never seen immigrant males killing pups, and there is no indication of a rise in the mortality of dependent young following the takeover of a group by new males. Why not? There is a simple reason. In contrast to langurs and many other primates, lactation does not prevent conception in meerkats and breeding females that have given birth typically conceive again within the next ten days. As a result, there is no benefit to males in killing dependent pups, for their mothers will already have conceived again or will shortly do so. Studies of the distribution of regular infanticide by males have now confirmed that it is restricted to animals where males have relatively short tenure in groups relative to the time it takes a mother to be ready to breed again.

*   *   *

The immigration of the Vivian males had important repercussions for the Whiskers females. Under the influence of increased sex hormones, most of them (including Flower) mated repeatedly with the new males. The sisters began to compete with each other as well as with Risca, chattering at each other and hip-slamming their rivals as they walked past. The frequency of aggression between females and the level of social tension both rose.

Risca initially held onto her position, but her sisters now rarely submitted to her and her ability to control them was gradually eroding. One day, the group became split into two halves while the animals were out foraging. When the two parties met up again the next day, Risca approached Vialli and threatened her, but, instead of moving away, Vialli whirled round and bit at her neck. Risca retaliated and the two cousins fought for several minutes.

Vialli was stronger and heavier and she eventually chased Risca away. This affected Risca's relationships with the other females, who repeatedly attacked her. Flower was among them and she now became dominant to Risca. After the fight with Vialli, Risca spent her time on the edges of the group. Though she continued to stay with the group, she slept alone at night and was usually the first animal up in the morning.

The three oldest females in the group were now Vialli, Wahine and Flower, all sisters. Vialli was five months older than Wahine who, in turn, was three months older than Flower. Dominance relationships between the three were uncertain and they chattered and hip-slammed each other, but eventually Vialli emerged as the winner and interactions between her and the others became more and more one-sided. Risca remained in the group but avoided her sisters and spent much of her time foraging on the periphery, while Vialli became more and more aggressive towards her. Eventually Vialli chased Risca out of the group. When she tried to rejoin her family, her brothers and sisters war danced at her and chased her if she came too close. She was forced to forage and sleep on her own.

After Vialli became the dominant female, her relationship with Zaphod changed. Whereas he had previously focused his attention on Risca, he now abandoned her and spent much of the time within a few yards of Vialli, displacing any of the other males that came too close to her. Dominant male meerkats commonly guard the breeding female in the group but, if she changes, rapidly transfer their attention to the new female. Though they are not always close to her, they are seldom far away and, during the weeks following a birth, when she is likely to conceive, they guard her closely. We collect skin samples from all pups born in the study area for DNA analysis and comparison of the genetic fingerprints of pups with those of their mother and possible fathers. Our results clearly show that, except in periods of social instability or when there is no immigrant male in the group, almost all pups born to dominant females are fathered by the resident dominant male. In contrast, pups born to subordinate females (who are commonly the daughters of the dominant male) are usually fathered by roving males from other groups, which explains the popularity of roving. Subordinate females mate readily with rovers and around a third of all subordinate litters are fathered by more than one male.

*   *   *

While dominant male meerkats can guard their partners effectively, and so father most of the offspring they produce, this is not the case in all mammal societies. When dominant males do not spend the whole day with females they cannot prevent them from mating with other males – and they often do so. For example, in the African ground squirrels that share the meerkats' ranges, dominant males defend territories overlapping the separate burrow systems of several females, and as they are not around all the time, they cannot prevent the females from mating with other males.

The promiscuity of female ground squirrels has important consequences. You cannot watch African ground squirrels for long without being struck by the enormous size of the males' balls. They droop down underneath their tails and often drag along the ground. When they are sitting down, males look as if they have brought along their own inflatable bouncer. When they walk, they have to waddle. It is one of those cases where it is hard to believe your eyes. Compared to ground squirrels, male meerkats have relatively small balls – though they are not poorly endowed.

Why the difference? Is it just that male meerkats need to run fast?

In fact, the relative size of the balls of males in different mammals is related to the risk that females will mate with several males within the same day or two. Where females often mate with several partners, receptive females commonly have sperm from several males in their reproductive tract at the same time. What is the best way for a male ground squirrel to make sure that it's his sperm that fertilises the female? Produce lots of them – and make sure they get as far up the female's reproductive tract as possible. To do this you need many sperm, large ejaculates and a long penis. Big balls and long penises are the result. Male meerkats, who are able to guard their females more effectively, do not need such elaborate tackle.

The relationship between mating systems and the relative size of balls occurs in other mammals, birds, insects and fish. Why do rams have enormous balls? Because ewes commonly mate with multiple partners. Why do male deer (usually) have relatively small ones? Because males can normally defend females effectively. Why, among the great apes, do male chimps have much larger balls relative to their body size than gorillas? Same story – male chimps live in groups that include multiple breeding males and females commonly mate with multiple partners, while gorillas live in harem groups and dominant males can defend their groups effectively against rivals.

And what about humans? Compared to chimps, we are poorly endowed, more like gorillas. This suggests that whatever mating system our immediate ancestors had, females seldom mated with multiple partners in each breeding attempt. But balls do not produce good fossils, so we have no way of knowing what the anatomy of our early ancestors looked like. Sex differences in body size among early hominids appear to have been greater than they are in modern man, suggesting that polygyny was more highly developed – so perhaps our early ancestors differed from us in other ways too. But it is unlikely that they came anywhere close to male ground squirrels.

*   *   *

Not long after evicting Risca, Vialli began to pick on her younger sister, Wahine, and chased her out of the group, too. Like Risca, Wahine stayed within sight of the group and the two cousins soon teamed up, foraging and sleeping together. But although this made foraging easier, their position was still precarious. With only two animals, a co-ordinated guarding system was impractical and both sisters regularly had to interrupt their digging to scan the horizon for danger. They had difficulty in catching prey effectively and they gradually lost weight. They began to wander more widely but soon encountered Lazuli. There was no way of opposing them and they were chased back into Whiskers' range. Without a territory of their own, they were at continual risk of attack and there could be no question of breeding.

Although social tension between the males eased after Zaphod became dominant, Whiskers now held few attractions for Izit, Genghis and Zazu and they left the group one by one, taking with them several of their younger brothers. Izit and two of his younger brothers left together. After leaving the group, they foraged for an hour and then set off to the north-west. After a few minutes, they came over the crest of a dune and saw meerkats digging below them. Approaching cautiously, they managed to get within a few metres before they were seen. One of the diggers heard something and spun round and the seven animals faced each other. It was Risca and Wahine together with two roving males from Vivian.

The animals sniffed each other but showed no aggression. They

soon settled down to forage and spent that night and the following day with each other. They stayed together for the next week,
gradually moving to the north-west of Whiskers' range where
there was a large area of flats with widely spaced camel thorns and
a large sleeping burrow. The area was part of the range of a group
called Balrog, who rarely visited it, and the burrows were partially
blocked with fallen sand. The animals set about clearing them and
soon they smelled clean and fresh. Over the following weeks, they
began to mark their range, testing the boundaries in all directions.

Though Risca was older than Wahine, she was in poor condition after the trauma of losing her status the previous month and
Wahine initially assumed the dominant position in the new group,
which we named Gattaca. But, three months later, when she was
foraging too intently, a martial eagle came low and fast over the
dune and carried Wahine off, leaving Risca as the dominant
female. Izit, too, had been affected by his removal from the dominant position in Whiskers and one of his younger brothers
initially achieved dominance in the group. But shortly after the
start of the New Year, a large rover from Vivian began hanging
around. Izit's mother, the dominant female of Vivian, had died,
leaving their father, Stinker, with only close female relatives in the
group. Stinker had started to search for a new group – and quickly
encountered his sons with two unrelated females. This was too
good an opportunity to pass up and he joined them, taking over
the dominant position and retaining it for several years until he
was finally replaced by Izit.

* * *

It was now approaching midsummer and the days were long
and hot. Vialli set about establishing her position in Whiskers.
With all her older sisters gone, Flower was closest to Vialli in

age and size and, after mating with several of the new males, both Vialli and Flower were pregnant and swelling fast. Though she had been guarded and fed by Vialli as a pup, Flower became the target of much of her older sister's aggression. When she dug deep for a scorpion or gecko, Vialli would pile into the hole, growling, and force her to give way. Though Flower avoided her sister whenever possible and grovelled to her when they met, Vialli took every opportunity to displace her, hip-slamming her whenever she passed.

One night in midsummer, Flower gave birth – but Vialli was there and killed her pups soon after they were born. Two days later, Vialli attacked Flower, biting at her genitals and the base of her tail. Flower curled up in a ball, trying to protect herself, but Vialli scrabbled at her, biting hard. The other members of the group crowded round but did nothing to interfere. Finally, Flower dashed away, with Vialli close behind her. Flower twisted and turned and eventually Vialli lost interest and returned to the group.

Flower sat and watched the group as they continued to forage. When they eventually moved on, she followed at a safe distance of around a hundred yards. Twice she tried to rejoin them and both times Vialli saw her and chased her away. As the sun went down, the group came to the large sleeping burrow in the middle of the acacia thicket where Flower had been born. As Flower watched, they settled down, grooming each other before going below ground for the night. When the last animal was gone, Flower left them and spent the night in an old porcupine hole close by.

That night, Vialli gave birth to her litter and emerged the next morning deflated and slim, with blood on her rear. Her litter was large and she was ravenous. The group went off to forage early, leaving Flower's younger sister, Smithers, and her cousin, Mi Julie, as babysitters. Once they had gone, Flower stole back to the burrow and joined Smithers and Mi Julie and the pups. She spent the rest of the day with them, immersing herself in their smell. When the group came back that evening, Vialli was well fed. She quickly rejoined the pups, ignoring Flower, and settled down to suckle them. Flower left her and went above ground to join the rest, who were spread around the burrow entrance. Without Vialli, the others readily tolerated Flower, who settled down to groom with Smithers. As the sun went down, they each went below and Flower eventually joined them.

Over the following weeks, Flower assisted the others in rearing Vialli's seven pups. After the loss of her own litter she was primed to lactate and she suckled them regularly. Like Smithers and Flower's cousins, Ugly and Mi Julie, she was a regular babysitter. The pups rapidly gained weight and started to forage with the group once they were three weeks old. There were two males, Tarzan and Big Will, and five females, Itchy, Scratchy, Thelma, Louise and Daisy.

Three weeks after her pups had begun to forage with the others, Vialli disappeared. We never found her body or her radio collar so she was probably taken by an eagle whose nest lay outside the range of our radios. The group continued to rear her pups and Flower, Ugly, Smithers and Mi Julie began to compete for dominance. Flower was larger than any of the others and won with little difficulty. She was now two years old, and for the first time in her life, she was the dominant female in the group.

6

THE TROUBLE WITH SISTERS

It was now early midsummer and the days were long and hot.
The meerkats got up early, sunned briefly and set off to forage.
Flower was almost two years old and was young for a dominant
female. After the eviction of her older sisters and the death of
Vialli, there were now only four other females over a year old in
the group. These were Smithers, Holly's last daughter, who was six
months younger than Flower, and Flower's three yearling cousins,
Ugly, Rydapuni and Mi Julie. In addition, Flower had five sub-
adult nieces in the group from the litter produced by Vialli the
previous November.

Zaphod was still the dominant male, and his relationship with
Flower changed. When Risca and Vialli had been dominant, he

had paid Flower little attention, but now he seldom let her out of his sight. Though they spent much of their time visiting other groups, Zaphod's brothers, who had immigrated with him from Vivian, were still in Whiskers. There was Zaphod's litter-mate Yossarian, now three and a half years old, and his younger brothers Genghis, Alexander, Attila, Phooey and Patas. The first three were litter-mates and almost exactly three years old, while Phooey and Patas were younger.

Following her rise in status, Flower's behaviour began to show subtle changes as the levels of sex hormones in her system rose. She became increasingly assertive in interactions with other members of Whiskers, playing an important role in determining the direction of movement of the group. She regularly displaced juveniles and other adults from holes that they had started to dig for prey and sometimes even stole prey they had caught. She also began to gain in size and weight.

Similar changes occur in females that attain dominant status in other co-operative breeders where a single female monopolises reproduction. As in meerkats, female naked mole-rats that have acquired the dominant position show higher levels of testosterone and become more aggressive, dominating other group members. They also increase in size allowing them to carry large litters of ten to fifteen pups. They do not participate much in the usual work of the colony and spend most of the time in the central breeding chamber, caring for their pups. Even more spectacular changes in growth and size occur in female termites that become queens. Like dominant female naked mole-rats, termite queens are fed by other members of the colony and play little role in collecting food, often increasing in size until they are many times their original weight, pumping out eggs that are raised by large numbers of workers. Since they no longer need to forage for themselves, they are not exposed to the same risks as workers and can live for twenty years or more. In contrast, dominant female meerkats forage for themselves and are vulnerable to the same risk of predation, with the result that their lifespans are similar to those of other adults.

After Vialli's death, all the adult females had mated and Flower, Smithers, Mi Julie and Ugly were pregnant. Almost exactly the same sequence of events that had occurred the previous breeding season was now repeated. Flower, the oldest and heaviest female, had conceived first and gave birth to her litter in early February. But Smithers, Mi Julie and Ugly were still pregnant and killed Flower's newborn pups. Three weeks later, Mi Julie gave birth – and her pups were killed by Smithers. Three days afterwards, Smithers gave birth – and her pups were killed by Ugly. Finally, five days later, Ugly gave birth to three pups. As the last litter born, these survived until they began to forage with the group. One might suppose that females would benefit by delaying conception when other females are in breeding condition, but meerkats do not appear to be capable of doing this.

Life was as precarious as ever and none of Ugly's pups lived for long. One day an eagle owl swooped low out of a camel thorn and carried off the largest pup. A few weeks later, Whiskers set out northwards and crossed the riverbed by the dead tree. They foraged in the short grass of the riverbed itself and then climbed the dunes leading up to the German's grave. They slipped through the rusty railings and examined the roots of the bushes that grew inside the enclosure, sheltered from browsing by goats and antelope. Moving on, they foraged along the edge of the riverbed. Scorpions and sun spiders were common here. Ugly's two remaining pups begged loudly and were fed by all the members of the group apart from Flower, who was still the dominant female.

The animals were hungry and there was no sentinel on duty.

Suddenly, another group of meerkats came charging down at them from the crest of the nearest dune. Unknown to Flower and her family, Lazuli had been foraging just the other side of the dune and had spotted them. There was no time to flee, and the two groups met and fought. Flower was attacked by two males and backed up to a tree root where she could keep them at bay. To her left, Zaphod was in the middle of a ball of biting animals. All across the face of the dune, pairs or trios of meerkats wrestled or chased each other. Cazanna, the new dominant female of Lazuli, dashed to and fro slashing, snarling and biting. She eventually came face to face with Flower – who turned and ran. The other members of her family disengaged and followed and the group bounded away, but one of Ugly's two remaining pups could not keep up and was left behind, between the fleeing group and their rivals. Cazanna was the first to reach the pup and grabbed it, biting it hard across the head and tossing it aside. She bounded on towards Whiskers, who continued to run.

For the next three months, Whiskers ran from almost every group they met. With the exception of Gattaca, all the neighbouring groups were bigger than they were and the situation was aggravated by the frequent absences of the larger males. The size of Whiskers' range slowly dwindled, forcing them to reuse the same foraging areas at regular intervals, and all their sleeping burrows were within strike of raiding parties from their neighbours. Lazuli now regularly used the Dune Flats and sometimes came as far east as the riverbed. In the south, Young Ones occupied the slopes of the dunes leading down to the South Flats while Elveera extended its range into the western part of Whiskers' territory. Vivian, the group from which Zaphod and his brothers had originally come, was now occupying the eastern part of Whiskers' range and sometimes ventured to the burrow in the acacia thicket where Flower had been born. Any pups they produced would be at the mercy of raids by their neighbours.

Autumn gave way to winter; the days shortened and the nights became cold. Whiskers continued to lose members. Ugly's last pup was killed by a goshawk and Patas, one of Zaphod's younger brothers who had joined Whiskers from Vivian, came back to the group badly wounded after he had been roving. He struggled to keep up with the group and was eventually left behind after a predator alarm. No one saw what eventually happened to him, but he failed to rejoin the group that evening.

The other males spent more and more time roving. Unless Whiskers could increase in size and extend its range, the future looked bleak. Fortunately, the winter was dry but mild and the meerkats' prey was not as deeply buried or as scarce as it had been the previous year. By midwinter, Flower was obviously pregnant and her belly was swelling. This time she was taking no chances. As her pregnancy advanced, she became more and more aggressive towards Smithers and her three nieces. She regularly took over the holes they were digging, growling and snapping. When she came across them while the group was foraging, she would hip-slam them and, sometimes, launch vicious attacks. All of the four subordinate females now spent most of their time on the edge of the group avoiding Flower – and when they met they chattered and grovelled.

Midway through July, Flower attacked Mi Julie and Ugly. Even though Whiskers was still a small group and was often displaced by larger neighbouring ones, she drove them away and, two days later, evicted Smithers and Rydapuni. The four outcasts teamed up and followed Whiskers each day. They tried several times to rejoin the group, but Flower chased them away repeatedly; soon the whole of Whiskers war danced at them whenever they appeared.

The four females were joined by three roving males from Lazuli and tried to establish a new group within part of Balrog's range. But Balrog drove them away and the males left them to search for better breeding opportunities elsewhere. The remaining females dispersed out of our study area and were not seen again. Rydapuni was the only exception. She persistently followed the members of Vivian group until, against all odds, they accepted her and she joined them – the only adult female we have ever seen who immigrated into an established breeding group.

A month later, Flower gave birth to her first litter of pups as a dominant female. This time, there were no other pregnant females in the group and all three pups survived their first month. There were two females, Badiel and Skinner, and one male, Stato, all fathered by Zaphod. Like Flower herself, the pups had a narrow escape when Elveera raided the breeding burrow and attacked them, but they were saved thanks to determined defence by the babysitters.

Evicting her sister and her nieces removed the threat that Flower's pups would be killed. However, it weakened Whiskers further and their neighbours continued to encroach on their range. It also reduced the number of helpers that could contribute to babysitting, pup feeding and sentry duty, so that the workload per individual increased. When they were not roving, Zaphod's adult brothers played an important role in caring for the pups, but they spent much of their time away and the other animals had to work hard. Flower was forced to make a substantial contribution to the care of her pups herself, slowing down the rate at which she could regain condition after the birth.

*   *   *

The regular eviction of older subordinate females by the dominant female is a crucial feature of meerkat society, for it is this practice that limits the size of groups and the number of breeding females. Older females are also evicted by dominant females in dwarf mongooses which consequently live in groups very like those of meerkats. In contrast, the larger banded mongoose lives in more egalitarian societies than meerkats. Most adult females breed and dominant females do not routinely evict subordinates, though parties of females leave established breeding groups from time to time and groups sometimes split. In parallel with our meerkat research, members of my group worked with banded mongooses in the Queen Elizabeth National Park in Western Uganda. Here, too, we were able to habituate groups to close observation and to train individuals to climb onto scales to be weighed – though the thicker vegetation meant that groups were harder to follow and their members were often difficult to see in the undergrowth.

The breeding system of the banded mongooses differed in several important ways from that of meerkats. Not only did most adult females breed each year but pregnancies were closely synchronised and breeding females usually gave birth on the same day. The likely reason for this became clear when we found that pups born out of synchrony rarely survived, probably because they were killed by other females. Presumably, the safest time for a mother to give birth is when all the other breeding females are similarly occupied and females cannot easily identify their own pups. However, many pups still die within a few days of birth and the size of litters emerging from the breeding burrow three to four weeks after the combined birth-day is much smaller than the total number of pups produced. Given the disadvantages of having potential competitors, it is not clear why dominant female banded mongooses do not evict older subordinates. One possibility is that, in the wetter savannahs and woodlands used by banded mongooses, food is more available than in the Kalahari. As a result, banded mongoose pups may not require the services of so many helpers to feed them and the pups of dominant females may not need to compete for access to helpers to the same extent as in meerkats, reducing the benefits to dominant females of suppressing reproduction by other females. In line with this explanation, each individual banded mongoose pup is fed primarily by a single 'dedicated' helper – in contrast to meerkats, where pups are fed by all group members.

*   *   *

As spring approached and the days lengthened and the weather warmed, Flower conceived again and produced her second litter of the season in early November, again fathered by Zaphod. This time there was one female, Mozart, and three males, Einstein, Freud and Shakespeare. The pups survived and were guarded and fed by the other group members. Ten days after giving birth, Flower came into oestrus again. A rover from Gattaca had been hanging around Whiskers and, this time, she mated with him when Zaphod's attention was diverted.

Although life quietens down after one female acquires the dominant position, she – like any absolute ruler – faces the continuous threat of being challenged for her position by one or more of her subordinates. If she loses, she will almost certainly be evicted – to face near-certain death. The changes that occur in females that acquire the dominant position play an important role in helping them to maintain their status, and to cover the costs of gestation and lactation. Testosterone, the quintessential male hormone, is closely associated with aggression and the need to respond to aggressive challenges. Its increased levels in dominant female meerkats is unusual and reflects the intense competition they face.

* * *

Meerkats are not the only social mammals where dominant females show high testosterone levels. Similar changes occur in female naked mole-rats and marmosets: as with meerkats, a single dominant female monopolises breeding in each group. They are also found in spotted hyenas, which live in clans of fifty or more animals; though multiple females breed in each clan, their breeding success is closely related to the female's dominance.

Perhaps the strongest evidence that competition is responsible for the development of high testosterone levels in females comes from research on Swiss cows. In the mountainous Vallais region of south-eastern Switzerland there is an unusual sport: cow fighting. Like many other social mammals, female cows kept together for any period of time develop well-defined dominance hierarchies through threats, aggression and occasional fights. Before farmers from the Vallais send their cattle up to high pastures for the summer months, they select their most competitive cows for organised cow fights. Two or three cows are put into a ring and encouraged to fight each other until there is a clear winner while everyone bets on the outcome. Cow fights have a long history and cattle have been selected for their competitiveness and aggression over many generations – and specific breeds of fighting cows have been developed. What unusual characteristics do they have? Unusually high testosterone levels in females.

High testosterone levels in females can affect the development of their offspring. In several of the species where adult females compete intensely and show high levels of testosterone, female genitalia are masculinised. Spotted hyenas are the most striking example: mature females develop an elongated clitoris that closely resembles the penis of males, so that, in the field, it can be difficult to tell males and females apart. Masculinisation comes with a high price tag for female hyenas. They give birth through their elongated clitoris, which has to stretch to allow the passage of a four-pound foetus. As a result, labour lasts an abnormally long time and many cubs born to first breeders die before birth.

Another striking characteristic of females in many co-operative breeders and other social species where competition between females is intense is that breeding females are commonly dominant to all other group members, including males. This is so widespread in the social insects that it is rarely remarked upon, but female dominance over males also occurs in many co-operative mammals, including naked mole-rats and meerkats. It is particularly clear in spotted hyenas, where females are larger and more frequently aggressive than males. When neighbouring clans defend their territories, it is females rather than males that are principally involved.

In spotted hyenas, the sex difference in aggressiveness extends back to the first weeks of life. Female hyenas commonly produce two cubs at a time, which are born with functional teeth. Within twenty-four hours of birth, they use their teeth to compete with each other for dominance, launching vicious attacks on their litter-mates. These are particularly intense where litters consist of two female cubs, while litters of male cubs or litters of mixed sex are (a bit) more peaceable. In all-female litters, the two cubs usually fight until one dies.

Female dominance over males may commonly be a by-product of intense competition between females – just as, in polygynous mammals, like red deer, male dominance over females may be a by-product of competition between males. However, it may also have specific benefits if it enhances the ability of females to compete with males for resources or allows them to control the identity of their males. For example, the dominance of female spotted hyenas over males may enhance the female's capacity to make sure that her dependent offspring can get access to resources.

* * *

By December, Flower was heavily pregnant and was scarcely able to run. She was not the only pregnant animal in the group: Itchy, Vialli's daughter, now two years old, was also pregnant and gave birth to her pups just before Christmas. Flower killed and ate them and, two days later, gave birth to her own litter consisting of two male pups, Cookie and Pookie, and one female, Sookie. With no other pregnant females there, the pups survived and all members of the group helped to rear them.

While Flower had secured her position by evicting all the other adult females, Zaphod still had five brothers in the group. All of them were unrelated to Flower, so any of them were potential mates. In late January, while Flower's three pups were still at the burrow, Yossarian, Zaphod's litter-mate, and Phooey, his younger brother, began to compete with each other for dominance. Phooey had begun his challenge by attempting to take half a millipede that Yossarian had found and the interaction escalated into an indecisive fight. Over the next month, the two scrapped occasionally without a clear win on either side.

In early January, the competition between Phooey and Yossarian escalated to involve the other brothers. Zaphod had played a leading role in a series of fights with Young Ones and was clearly exhausted. His younger brother, Alexander, now decided that this was an opportunity to launch his own bid for the dominant position and attacked Zaphod. The pair rolled around on the sand, slashing and biting, while the rest of the group looked on. They broke apart and Alexander briefly chased Zaphod, who turned and bit him in the neck. They rolled over and over, sand flying in all directions. Eventually, Alexander had had enough and he broke and ran. His front leg was dragging, opened up from the shoulder to the elbow by a deep slash from Zaphod's canines.

As Zaphod rested after the fight with Alexander, Yossarian attacked him. Yossarian was smaller than Zaphod and Zaphod soon buried his teeth in Yossarian's face and dragged him around the group. Yossarian emerged from the fight with a deep slash over his left eye, which scarred him for the rest of his life. Later that day, Phooey, the heaviest but youngest of the brothers, returned from visiting Young Ones. Zaphod was clearly exhausted – and Phooey immediately attacked him. A further fight followed but, though heavier, Phooey lacked the skill and determination of his older brother and was quickly beaten.

Though he had been convincingly vanquished and was still bleeding, Yossarian now attacked Zaphod again and the brothers rolled over and over in the sand, broke, chased each other and fought again. This time the outcome was less clear-cut and a further fight followed before the group eventually slept for the night. When they emerged the next morning, the atmosphere was tense and the brothers avoided each other. Soon after they had started foraging, Yossarian again attacked Zaphod and once more there was a series of brawls. This time, Yossarian emerged as the winner. He assumed the dominant position, and, as the group moved off, he remained close to Flower, while Zaphod returned to the burrow and, uncharacteristically, spent the day babysitting Flower's pups.

With four adult brothers still in the group, Yossarian's position was insecure and he was suspicious and aggressive. For several weeks following the battle, Alexander was scarcely able to walk and was the victim of constant bullying by Yossarian. Yossarian's brothers spent much of their time roving – but when they returned, Yossarian would attack them viciously before allowing them to rejoin the group. For several days, Attila had a loose flap of skin on the back of his head where Yossarian had grabbed him.

As summer faded into autumn, the weather cooled and the days began to draw in. Without most of the adult males regularly foraging in the group, Whiskers were still at a disadvantage when they encountered their neighbours. Relationships between the resident males were tense. Following his displacement from the dominant position by Yossarian, Zaphod initially retained his dominance over the males, though they became more resistant to his threats. Eventually, Alexander and Dangerous Dave, the two-year-old son of Artemis, both attacked Zaphod. After a lengthy three-cornered fight, Zaphod was chased across the group by the other two. That night, he slept alone at a bolthole close to their sleeping burrow, though he rejoined them the next morning.

In one of the narrow valleys above the South Flats, Whiskers encountered a large Cape cobra. It was early in the morning and the snake was still hunting, though it quickly curled up defensively when the meerkats approached. Zaphod saw it first and backed away with his fur and tail up, making spitting calls. The snake soon attracted the attention of the rest of the group, who formed a half-circle round it with their fur and tails up. The adult males led the display, approaching the cobra more closely than the rest, lunging at it from a safe distance and making spit calls. The snake raised its head and spread its hood and struck at Zaphod, who leapt back. The cobra then decided that it was time to move and promptly sidled off towards the shelter of a bush, but the meerkats surrounded it and blocked its path. It reared again and struck at them, but they kept out of reach. After a further ten minutes of intense mobbing, the females, who had been hanging back in the attack, began to lose interest and the snake was able to slide away into the shade of an acacia bush, where it quickly found a hole between the roots and escaped below ground.

After producing her last litter in January, Flower had not conceived again but her two subordinate nieces, Scratchy and Thelma, were heavily pregnant. Scratchy gave birth to her litter in early March and this time Flower was not pregnant and did not kill the pups. For two days the pups survived and the group left a babysitter to guard them but, on the third day, the group left no babysitters and, that night, they slept at a different burrow. Scratchy remained with the group and her pups were abandoned. Three weeks later, Thelma produced her litter and again, the pups survived but were abandoned by the group a few days later.

The days shortened and the nights became colder as the summer faded into autumn. During April and May, Whiskers had lost three members. First Sookie, the female pup from Flower's third litter, was killed by a goshawk. Then, two weeks later, Freud, one of the juveniles from Flower's second litter, disappeared, followed three days later by Cookie, the second male pup from her third litter. Dangerous Dave, Artemis' son, took to roving and eventually left the group permanently. The other adult males, excluding Yossarian, also spent much time visiting other groups in a band – so they were often absent when Whiskers encountered their neighbours. As a result, Whiskers continued to run from all the neighbouring groups apart from Gattaca, and their range remained small. As winter approached and the camel thorns gradually shed their leaves, they were forced to move further and further each day and became thin and hungry. At night they curled up together in a large ball but, even deep underground, temperatures were low and they lost more and more weight.

Despite the deaths and emigrations, Whiskers had increased in size during the year and now numbered nineteen animals. Flower was three years old and, as the difference in age and experience between her and the other females had increased, her capacity to control their breeding attempts had improved and the frequency of such attempts declined. As a result, Flower's last three litters of pups had not faced the same risk of infanticide as had her litters of the previous season. Of the ten pups she had produced during the year, all had survived their first month and six were still living. The pups born to her first litter of the season, Badiel, Stato and Skinner, were now large enough to play an important role in guarding and feeding her second litter. By next season, the living pups born in her second litter, Einstein, Mozart and Shakespeare, would be ready to help too, reducing the need for Flower herself to feed the pups and allowing her to regain condition rapidly after breeding.

7

FLOWERPOWER

The next winter was long and cold. In early July 2003, the wind blew from the south and temperatures were below freezing each morning. The meerkats got up late and spent a long time sunning before they left for the day's march. Food was scarce and they spent much of their time feeding on beetles and millipedes. Once again, the desert looked parched and faded. Sudden winds stirred dust clouds or small tornadoes that wound their way across the South Flats.

Flower was now over three years old and was clearly dominant to all the other members of Whiskers. When she was foraging and came across another group member who had dug a deep hole and was on the point of extracting a large prey item, she would often barge them aside and occupy the hole. She would growl until they gave up, leaving her to extract the food without having to put in the actual effort. When her juvenile sons or daughters finally captured an animal that was difficult to handle – a long, pink burrowing skink or a large millipede – Flower would appear and grab the food. Sometimes this led to protracted tugs of war as Flower tried to wrench the food free from their jaws. Burrowing skinks were long and tough and Flower would sometimes grab hold of one end and drag a protesting juvenile, attached to the other end, for several yards. To break her children's grip, she sometimes circled, swinging them around her. Even Yossarian suffered from Flower's depredations.

Eventually, in late August, temperatures began to rise again and the first green shoots appeared on the camel thorns. Crowned plovers began displaying noisily on the flats. Lilac-breasted rollers reappeared on the tops of dead trees or flew in circles giving a creaking call and exposing their turquoise underwings at intervals. Small, green swallow-tailed bee-eaters hawked for insects around the shrubs. The springbok produced their lambs, which followed the adults awkwardly on spiky legs but still could show remarkable speed when alarmed.

Flower was pregnant, but food was scarce and she was too light to be able to breed successfully. She aborted her offspring and ate the foetuses while they were still warm. However, with the rising temperature, insects were breeding and the meerkats' food supply was increasing rapidly. At night, clouds of small moths fluttered around our lights. Flower rapidly gained weight and soon conceived again.

The joys of spring were not lost on the males, who renewed their visits to prospect for receptive females in other groups.

Vialli's yearling sons, Tarzan and Big Will, now nearly two, joined the older males on their first foray. They travelled south until they encountered Young Ones, who were foraging busily in the dunes to the north of the South Flats. Young Ones saw them and began to war dance, but the males kept their distance and were gradually ignored. They waited for an opportunity to get close and approach any female that lagged behind. Alexander slipped away from his brothers and ran low to the ground from bush to bush, hiding from Young Ones resident males. A two-year-old female had been on sentry duty and had become separated from her family as the rest of the group foraged on. As she climbed down from her perch, Alexander ran towards her, chattering submissively. She stopped and the two animals sniffed each other. The female ran a few yards and Alexander followed her, mounted her and they mated quickly before she ran back to join the group and Alexander rejoined his brothers.

Tarzan and Big Will watched Alexander's performance closely. Another female was foraging on the outskirts of the group and they tentatively approached her. Tarzan was more enthusiastic and bounded up to her and she turned, sensing an intruder, her hair and tail up. Tarzan was unsure of himself and stood looking at her, not realising the danger he was in. The female's alarm had not gone unnoticed and five adult Young Ones males charged him. Tarzan turned and ran, but he was not quick enough and the leading male caught him and sank his teeth in his shoulder. Off balance, he fell and all five males piled in on him, slashing and biting. Tarzan curled up in a tight ball to avoid having his stomach and genitals bitten. His brothers ran, making no attempt to rescue him. Eventually, the Young Ones males lost interest and Tarzan was able to escape, but with serious bite wounds to his head, legs and genitals.

Tarzan limped away on his own and made it back to the Whiskers' sleeping burrow, where the group found him when they returned for the night. The others sniffed and groomed him, licking his wounds. His injuries gradually healed in the course of the next month but, following this experience, he seldom joined the other males when they went roving and he spent most of his time with the group. Tarzan was lucky, for roving male meerkats are quite commonly killed if they approach breeding groups too closely and get caught.

*   *   *

Similar events happen with many other mammals. Male lions that stray into the territories of neighbouring prides are likely to be attacked and are not uncommonly killed by the resident males. Some of the most extreme violence between males occurs in chimpanzees, our closest relatives. In chimpanzee societies, females have separate ranges which they share with dependent and adolescent young, while groups of related males jointly defend larger territories, incorporating the ranges of many females. Relationships between males from neighbouring communities are hostile and male groups will readily kill those from adjoining territories if they can, possibly because this weakens their rivals and allows them to extend their boundary. Parties of male chimps go on raids into their neighbours' territories to search for victims. Normally, travelling chimps advertise their presence and vocalise frequently but, on raids, males are intent and silent and appear to be on the lookout for males that are on their own or in smaller parties. When they find them, they attack with great ferocity, often either killing them outright or leaving them so badly wounded that they do not survive for long.

It is sometimes suggested that, apart from man, chimpanzees are the only animal that engages in warfare. However, there is little difference between the behaviour of chimpanzees and that of many other animals where groups defend territories against their neighbours. In many social ants, larger colonies probe the defences of smaller neighbouring colonies of the same species and send out specialised raiding parties consisting primarily of soldier castes to attack them if their defences are weak or colony size is small. As a result, many small colonies are wiped out by their neighbours and only a small proportion of starter colonies make it through the early stages of development and become established breeding colonies. In meerkats, groups that go on invasive excursions routinely inspect sleeping burrows when they come across them and if they find pups and babysitters in them, nearly always attack in an attempt to kill them, and are often successful. It may be that their excursions are often organised specifically for this purpose.

* * *

A few weeks after the attack on Tarzan, the roving males had better luck. The dominant female of Young Ones was pregnant and had evicted three of her older daughters, who lagged behind the group at a safe distance. On a visit to Young Ones, Zaphod, Alexander and Phooey saw these three females and approached them cautiously. The two parties sniffed each other, and groomed briefly. Then the oldest of the sisters bounded away. Alexander ran after her, caught her and the pair mated. The brothers spent the rest of the day with the sisters, mating freely but, in the evening, they returned to Whiskers. Next day they visited the same area again, but the three sisters had disappeared.

* * *

When male and female meerkats mate, copulation always appears to occur with the females' co-operation. This is by no means universal – forced copulation is common in many mammals, including chimpanzees and orang-utans. In chimpanzees and macaques, dominant males will punish females for refusing their advances, or for consorting with subordinate males, by attacking them, sometimes causing substantial injuries. In Soay sheep, gangs of males chase oestrus ewes until they can run no further. Then individual males mate with them in turn. Rams are often so fired up they find it difficult to wait and, while one male is mounting the female, he is commonly mounted by another male, who may be mounted by a third, who is sometimes mounted by a fourth, all busy thrusting away.

Whether cases of forced copulation in animals should be referred to as rape is a moot point. Females commonly seek to avoid forced mating attempts and are sometimes injured and occasionally killed when multiple males try to mate with them. However, it is widely suggested that the trauma they undergo cannot compare with that suffered by humans who are raped and that describing animals as raping each other undervalues the horror of rape in humans. As a result, most scientists prefer to use 'forced copulation' instead.

Why do male meerkats rarely or never need to force females to copulate with them? One likely reason is that dominant males can usually control access to breeding females and so do not need to be in a rush to mate. Forced copulation in mammals most commonly occurs where subordinate males need to mate rapidly before a dominant male shows up and displaces them. Under these circumstances, they may be able to increase their breeding success by making it dangerous for females to refuse to mate with them. So long as it is not fatal, any injury that a female sustains as a consequence will have little or no drawback for the male and the threat or risk of injury to females may increase the chance that females will comply rapidly. In contrast, where dominant males control access to females, they do not need to mate rapidly and can wait until females are ready to co-operate.

* * *

By mid-October, Flower was obviously pregnant and so was her niece Scratchy, the largest of Vialli's daughters. Flower began to direct regular aggression at Scratchy and finally evicted her. A week later, she drove out two of her other nieces, Itchy and Thelma, while Louise and Daisy, her youngest two nieces, remained in the group. The three evicted females hung around the group and tried to rejoin it, but Flower chased them away repeatedly.

After they had been evicted, the females tailed Whiskers. They were not in such danger or as stressed as solitary evicted meerkats and Scratchy, instead of aborting her litter, produced her pups in one of the group's regular sleeping burrows on the South Flats. The females foraged around the burrow during the day and were still there when Whiskers arrived back in the evening. Whiskers wardanced and drove them away, but did not kill the pups and, over the next few days, Scratchy returned to suckle them as soon as Flower and the rest of the group had left to forage. However, there were not enough group members to allow them to leave a babysitter, and two days later a visiting yellow mongoose killed the pups. After this, the three sisters left the study area and we never discovered their fate. Louise and Daisy initially remained in Whiskers but, soon after, they were both driven out by Flower and they subsequently disappeared, too.

All the remaining females in the group were now Flower's

daughters and most of the resident males were her sons, with the exception of Big Will, her nephew, and the four immigrant males, Yossarian, Zaphod, Attila and Alexander. Dominant females are more likely to evict older and heavier subordinate females than younger and lighter ones – and also pregnant ones. Kinship, too, is important and they evict more distant relatives – nieces, aunts and grandchildren – at an earlier age than their sisters or their offspring.

Overt conflict between females is less common in groups that are led by well-established dominant females. Subordinate females less often conceive and the risk of infanticide is lower, so that they are less likely to attempt to breed and tend to be more generous as helpers. In addition, as the disparity in age between dominant and subordinate females increases, dominants can control subordinates more effectively, restricting their growth and sexual development. As a result, the annual breeding success of dominant females increases the longer they have held the dominant position until, towards the end of their lifespan, their capacity to control the other females in the group eventually declines.

* * *

In early December, Flower was pregnant again and gave birth to the fourth litter she had produced as dominant female. This time there were three female pups, Kinkaju, Rocket Dog and Super Furry Animal, and one male, Ragga Muffin. The pups were healthy and Flower left them in charge of her two oldest daughters, Mozart and Badiel. By the end of the day, Mozart had begun to lactate and, as the pups' needs grew and they begged hungrily, Badiel did so too. All four pups survived to emergence and began to forage with the group in early January.

A week after she had produced her litter, Flower came into oestrus. She became uncharacteristically playful and joined her sub-adult offspring in games of tag and chase. By late January, she was noticeably pregnant again and so, too, were Mozart and Badiel. Her two daughters were still pregnant when Flower gave birth to her fifth litter at the beginning of February. This time, Flower produced three females, Monkulus, Lucky and Armanita Ditch, and two males, Pozzo and Zarathustra. Though they were pregnant, neither of her daughters killed Flower's litter and all the pups survived to forage with the group.

Three weeks later, Badiel produced one female pup, De La Soul, and three males, Flava Flav, Bad Boy Bubby and the sickly Arrested Development. Badiel's pups were less than two weeks old when Flower's were ready to forage with the group and Flower led Whiskers to a new sleeping burrow. But Badiel managed to carry her pups one by one to the new burrow and the whole litter survived. A few days later, Mozart gave birth, but the group had now resumed its normal practice of changing sleeping burrows every two or three days and the newborn pups were abandoned.

*   *   *

Throughout the breeding season, Yossarian's four brothers, Zaphod, Alexander, Phooey and Attila, continued to go roving regularly, visiting all the neighbouring groups in turn. Often they took Big Will and, sometimes, Tarzan, now fully recovered. Occasionally, Flower's three yearling sons, Stato, Einstein and Pookie, went too. The dominant female of Young Ones had recently died and her mate, left without unrelated females in the group, had emigrated, leaving them without a breeding male. Several of the sons of the dominant female were still in the group and prevented roving males from elsewhere from immigrating, although they made no attempt to mate with their sisters or to guard them closely. As a result, Zaphod was able to mate with Veda, the new dominant female, and her sisters repeatedly and he spent many happy days hanging around Young Ones.

Each time his brothers returned from roving, Yossarian attacked them. Alexander first became the focus of Yossarian's paranoia and was beaten up repeatedly and forced to spend the day on the periphery of the group. Next it was Phooey's turn but, unlike Alexander, he fought back and Zaphod joined them. After a struggle, Yossarian beat them though Phooey was substantially heavier than he was. The adult males continued to spend much of their time visiting other groups and Phooey, Attila and Tarzan left the group permanently.

Yossarian maintained his role as dominant male throughout the breeding season. When Flower was in oestrus, he guarded her jealously and would not let the other males approach her. However, his life now took another turn. In late February, Alexander could stand Yossarian's attacks no longer and, when Yossarian approached him, growling, he growled back and tried to bite his face. The two brothers fought, rolling over and over in the sand, then broke and fought again. Yossarian emerged as the clear winner – but both were tired and Alexander was still not fully subdued. All day they growled at each other when they met.

That afternoon, Zaphod returned from a successful day with the dominant female of Young Ones and found Yossarian and Alexander still sparring. Seizing his chance, he attacked Yossarian and there was a protracted fight. Eventually, Zaphod pinned down Yossarian and bit him repeatedly in the face and shoulders, forcing him to curl up to avoid further injury. Zaphod emerged as the clear winner and took back the dominant role in Whiskers, which he had lost just over a year previously. He marked every burrow he came across with his bulging anal glands and guarded Flower jealously, while Yossarian resumed his life on the periphery of the group.

* * *

Winter was now approaching and, though Flower and Mozart were both pregnant, neither had the reserves to rear a litter and they both aborted. Once again, the days shortened and the desert became dusty and lifeless. One crisp, blue, cloudless morning followed another as the meerkats spent full days foraging for scarce resources.

As before, Whiskers regularly encountered their neighbours. Although they had lost several group members and the older males were often away roving, all the neighbouring groups had lost members too, and Whiskers were now no smaller than Young Ones, Elveera or Lazuli. In mid-October they encountered Young Ones in the dunes above the South Flats and chased them back to their own range. Two weeks later, they crested a dune in the west of their range and found Elveera foraging below them. They attacked immediately, but three Elveera females fought with Flower, who ran and the rest of Whiskers followed. Ten days later, they met Lazuli on the Dune Flats, war danced and chased them back almost to the Big Dune. After this victory, Whiskers gradually began to reuse the western part of their original range, which they had abandoned during the previous two years.

8

LOCAL HERO

In May 2004, Flower began her third breeding season as a dominant female. All the adult females in the group were her daughters and her position was secure. She was pregnant and so, too, were her eldest daughters, Mozart and Badiel. Flower had conceived first and would give birth before the others, so there was a real risk that her pups would be killed by her daughters, but, this time, she made no attempt to evict them. In June she gave birth to her sixth litter, consisting of two female pups, Hawkeye and Cruise, and two males, Logan and Mitch. Flower's pregnant daughters did not kill her pups, which developed rapidly. Twelve days after Flower had hers, Mozart gave birth to a litter of four which also survived. Two weeks later, Badiel produced a further three – so there were now three litters of pups in the burrow, all at different stages of development.

In September, there was a new arrival in the life of the Whiskers group. The characteristics that make Kalahari meerkats such a suitable species for research on social behaviour – the open habitat that they live in, their readiness to accept and ignore observers, and their complex social lives – make them an ideal subject for wildlife filmmakers. They are also unusually appealing, with their dark-rimmed eyes on the front of their faces and their tendency to stand upright using their tails as a support. Since the beginning of the study, filmmakers had visited us at intervals. The *National Geographic* sent a team to shoot a half-hour television film, and the BBC did another. David Attenborough visited for footage for one of his mega-series and the obligatory shot with a meerkat on his shoulder.

Then one day my phone rang. It was Caroline Hawkins from Oxford Scientific Films. They were considering making an animal soap opera on meerkats that followed the lives of individuals. Could I tell her where it could best be shot? I had seen a previous programme of hers that had followed the life histories of individual baboons and been impressed. In addition, it was not difficult to see the parallels between human soap operas and the complex social lives of meerkats. Both closely resemble a protracted game of snakes and ladders where the leading characters mix romance and co-operation with vicious competition.

I told Caroline that our study area was the ideal location and suggested that she should visit us. She came to the Kalahari and we discussed a series of programmes that would follow the life stories of individuals from one of the groups. I agreed to collaborate on the grounds that the films would tell meerkat life as it really is – a mixture of extreme co-operation and ruthless conflict. Not too many cuddly images, a limit to the degree of anthropomorphic interpretation and, above all, no claims that meerkat society provides a model for humans. Recent documentaries about animals had been getting mushier and mushier and we both felt that we could provide something more realistic.

In September, the film crew arrived to start shooting. We directed them to Whiskers since they were particularly well habituated, and taught them to recognise individual animals and interpret their behaviour. For the next six months, a succession of crews visited the group each day. The meerkats found the camera teams little more alarming, or interesting, than they found us. Sometimes they sniffed the strange equipment they carried. When the cameramen lay flat to get low-angle shots, one or more of the meerkats sometimes climbed onto their backs. They would sometimes stare at the large dark eye at the end of the camera lens or tentatively approach and sniff at the lens. If the sun was behind them, they were able to see their own reflection in the element and would stare at it with interest. On one occasion, I watched Stinker, the aptly named dominant male of Gattaca, sniff the camera lens with interest and then whirl around and smear his large wet anal gland right across the element, leaving a sticky brown mark on the lens.

The film team erected fixed cameras at some of the Whiskers sleeping burrows, but, because the animals changed burrows on a regular basis, these were of little use and all the film that was eventually used was taken by mobile cameramen. Over the next six months, the team obtained footage of the social lives of the meerkats that has few parallels in animal documentaries. They filmed babysitting, pup feeding and guarding from a few feet away. They could set up cameras so close to sentinels that the camera's reflection is sometimes visible in their pupils. They filmed eviction and infanticide and were able to follow individual meerkats after they had been evicted from the group. They documented raids, war dances and extended battles between groups as well as potentially lethal (and entirely natural) attacks by snakes, eagles and owls.

When the programmes came to be made, the footage had to be edited, for even the busy lives of meerkats would not be interesting watching if filmed in real time. However, the daily events in Whiskers were sufficiently dramatic that there was little need to fabricate a story, and the programme closely followed the events in Whiskers that season. In most cases, the films used the same names for individual animals that we did, but some sequences of events had to be simplified to avoid tedious repetition and so some characters in the programmes ended up as composites of several real meerkats.

Caroline and I went over the scripts for the programmes together. We were both keen that they should tell the story of the group from the animals' point of view, in order to engage the audience. I was prepared to accept descriptions of the animals as worried, anxious or aggressive, because there are obvious actions that reflect these states, but I crossed out adjectives such as sad, jealous, or loving since there is no way to identify emotions of this kind in animals in the field. Perhaps Yossarian did feel jealous whenever he saw Zaphod mating with Flower – but we had no possible way of knowing. Eventually Caroline and I reached a compromise over the scripts where I felt that the level of anthropomorphism was acceptable. The programmes aired in the United States and rapidly established a much larger audience than anyone had expected.

* * *

Throughout the breeding season, Whiskers went on with their lives as usual, ignoring the camera teams that visited them each day. Flower's sixth litter still had not emerged from the burrow when the filming started. Since Mozart and Badiel also had younger litters of pups in the same burrow, the situation was complex and it was not clear what the outcome would be. On this occasion, Flower made no attempt to lead Whiskers away from the breeding burrow when her pups were three weeks old and the group continued to use the same burrow each night for five weeks. As the days passed, the cavities and tree roots within a day's journey of the burrow had all been explored and the meerkats gained less and less weight each day. The fleas using the burrow multiplied and the meerkats spent more and more time scratching themselves and grooming each other.

Eventually, Yossarian attempted to initiate a move. With Shakespeare, Flower's two-year-old son, and Kinkaju, Flower's yearling daughter, he had remained behind at the breeding burrow to babysit the pups when the rest of the group left to forage. Yossarian went below ground and reappeared with one of Mozart's pups, still only two weeks old. He carried the pup twenty metres from the burrow, left it on the sand and then returned underground. The two other babysitters were evidently disconcerted and, after some indecision, Shakespeare fetched the pup and carried it back to the burrow.

Six days later, Yossarian tried again. Shortly after the main group had left to forage, he began moving pups up from the breeding burrow and then led Flower's pups away to another one half a kilometre away. Alarmed by the pups' cries, the group returned and there was a period of confusion as Badiel and Mozart tried to transfer the younger pups to the new burrow. Mozart successfully managed to lead her four pups there, though one could not keep up and was abandoned, while Badiel carried all three of her eight-day-old pups across to the new burrow.

Four days later, Flower's pups began foraging with the group and were soon joined by the others. Because they were nearly six weeks old, they were relatively mobile and the two younger litters of pups continuously got left behind, crying loudly as the group foraged. Their mothers did their best to encourage them to keep up and carry them when they were tired but they were unable to keep track of them all of the time and first Badiel and then Mozart lost a pup. The rest survived and grew rapidly as soon as they started to be fed by the group. Mozart now had one surviving son, Spud, and one daughter, Tina Sparkle, while Badiel had two surviving sons, Maladoy and Jogu.

After Zaphod had regained his position, he was more tolerant of his brothers than Yossarian had been and relationships between the males were relaxed. Alexander and Big Will continued to visit the neighbouring groups, sometimes taking Flower's older sons with them, but Zaphod now no longer joined them. There was still no immigrant breeding male in Young Ones and both Big Will and Alexander mated with the dominant female as well as with several of her sisters. Eventually, Alexander was accepted by the group and became her breeding partner and the resident breeding male of Young Ones, while Big Will moved on to try his luck elsewhere. Einstein, Flower's most precocious son, initially joined Alexander in Young Ones, but finally left the area as part of a splinter group.

Towards the end of October, Flower began to direct regular aggression at her oldest daughters, Mozart and Badiel, and a month later she evicted them both from the group. As before, the two sisters hung around within sight of Whiskers and repeatedly tried to rejoin the group, but Flower chased them away each time they did so and they were forced to forage and sleep on their own.

*   *   *

One day, when the group had been foraging in the eastern part of the range, they came to a grove of small camel thorns growing in the valley between two dunes. The outside tree had a hole between its roots and, when Kinkaju investigated this, something moved inside the entrance. Kinkaju backed away, hair and tail up, giving spit calls, and the rest of the group joined her. The hole was occupied by a large puff adder which clearly felt threatened by the meerkats and was coiled and ready to strike.

The meerkats mobbed the snake, pressing close together and nodding and spitting at it. As usual, the males were the most active mobbers and formed the front line. The snake struck once, and they all jumped back, then pressed forward again. In the crush, the animals at the front got pushed closer to the snake and became tightly packed, so their room for manoeuvre was limited. Shakespeare was at the front and lunged and spat at the snake. It struck again and this time, it buried its fangs in Shakespeare's left shoulder, delivering a large dose of venom. It immediately struck again, catching his left hind leg. Shocked, Shakespeare escaped from the mobbing group and stood half-stunned and in obvious pain. Eventually, the group moved off and Shakespeare followed them in a daze. As the poison spread, he found it harder and harder to walk on his injured leg. Eventually, he lay down in the shade of a bush and was left behind.

After resting for half an hour, Shakespeare set off, no longer trying to rejoin the group but heading back for the sleeping burrow. His left leg dragged uselessly and he was forced to walk on three legs. Throughout the afternoon, he moved by fits and starts and it was beginning to get dark when he eventually reached the burrow. The rest of the family had been back for a while and were preparing to sleep. They crowded around Shakespeare, sniffing and rubbing him and Kinkaju groomed his injured leg. After the rest had gone below for the night, he slowly joined them.

Next morning, Shakespeare did not emerge from the burrow with the rest of the group, who left to forage and slept at a different burrow that evening. But, though badly injured, he was not dead and, the next day, dragged himself up to the mouth of the burrow and lay in the sun. Badiel and Mozart, who had been evicted by Flower ten days before, turned up at the burrow and found Shakespeare there. The sisters sniffed at him and groomed him and, that night, the three slept together.

The day after, Shakespeare surfaced with the others but he was still shivering and uncoordinated and he did not leave the burrow. The muscle on his left leg was beginning to waste around the bone. The following day he was much the same and was clearly very hungry. He foraged in the vicinity of the burrow, walking on three legs and falling over regularly. However, he managed to find several grubs and a number of beetles and gradually his strength returned, though his left leg was black and shrivelled and he continued to walk on three legs.

The next day, Shakespeare was foraging with Badiel and Mozart when Whiskers appeared. The two sisters made themselves scarce, but Shakespeare joined the group and was sniffed and groomed all over. Over the following weeks, he regained his strength and began to take his share of social activities, guarding, babysitting and feeding pups – all on three legs. Instead of becoming infected, his injured leg began to recover muscle tone, the fur grew back and he was more mobile. Eventually it healed completely.

In early December, Flower gave birth to her seventh litter of pups. This time there were two female pups, Petra and Popkat, and two males, Machu Picchu and Ningaloo. After the pups were born, Mozart repeatedly attempted to rejoin Whiskers, grovelling to Flower and attempting to groom her, and eventually Flower accepted her presence. Mozart began to lactate and helped Flower to rear the pups, who started to forage with the group. Shortly after this, Shakespeare disappeared from the group and may either have dispersed or been killed by a predator.

* * *

Whiskers' numbers were now up to thirty and they were one of the largest groups in the area. This increase had several advantages. There were many individuals to guard, so they spent more time on sentry duty, providing a more effective early warning system of potential danger. When the helpers babysat Flower's pups, there were more animals to contribute, so that the contribution of each was reduced. Pup feeding, too, was spread over more individuals so that everyone was able to retain a larger proportion of the food that they found, and their body weight increased and they grew faster. The pups received more food, grew more quickly, became independent faster and showed higher rates of survival.

As their numbers increased, Whiskers became more and more successful in encounters with their neighbours. They usually won skirmishes with Young Ones and Elveera and extended their range to the south. Though they still lost to Lazuli as frequently as they won, they no longer ran away immediately they met them and Lazuli gradually moved away to the west, leaving Whiskers to occupy all the land between the river and the Big Dune.

The splinter groups that budded off from Whiskers and made their way out into the wider world of the Kalahari also became larger as the number of animals in Whiskers increased. In each of her recent breeding attempts, Flower had evicted several females at the same time, who had then joined up and either dispersed together as a group or eventually found their way back into Whiskers. Single meerkats that disperse almost certainly die: roving males may mate with them but do not stay with them and, without other individuals, they cannot start to breed successfully. Not only are large splinter groups safer and less stressed in the weeks after they have been evicted, but males are also much more likely to stay with them and they have a much better chance of establishing themselves as a new breeding group. As a result, the number of Flower's children in the wider population increased.

With thirty animals foraging over a broad front, it was often difficult for all of Whiskers to remain in contact. When a guard gave an alarm call, some would run to one bolthole while others would run to another. When the danger passed, the two halves of the group sometimes set off in different directions and only met up again at the sleeping burrow. Temporary splits became more and more frequent.

In early January, soon after Flower's pups had begun to forage with the group, Yossarian was on sentry duty when he spotted a martial eagle approaching low over the dunes. He gave the alarm and all the animals ran for shelter. Flower, one of her pups, Zaphod, Mozart and four of the younger ones ran to one bolthole while the rest of the group ran to another. The eagle passed on without attacking them and the meerkats gradually relaxed. Flower was intent on foraging and Zaphod guarded her closely. They moved off to the west, oblivious of the fact that the rest had gone in the opposite direction and soon the two parts of Whiskers were out of direct contact. Eventually, Flower and Zaphod realised that their party had become separated and they ran about nervously, inspecting all the boltholes and burrows in the immediate area. In spite of their efforts, the two groups of meerkats slept in different burrows that night. In the confusion, Popkat lagged behind and was abandoned.

While Flower, Zaphod and the rest of their party searched for the remainder of the group, the other meerkats were initially less disturbed. However, after a while they realised that Flower was no longer there and became agitated and searched the usual bolt-holes and the nearest burrow. During the afternoon, there were several aggressive interactions between Flower's older daughters, and Super Furry Animal, who was already pregnant, began to assert her dominance. Yossarian was the most dominant of the males, but because he had been in the group when Super Furry Animal was conceived he showed no sexual interest in her, and continued to go roving with the other males. With Flower gone, there was nothing to prevent Badiel from rejoining Whiskers and she quickly did so, immediately displacing Super Furry Animal and assuming the dominant position.

The two halves of Whiskers continued to forage in the separate parts of the range and both adopted the normal routine of sunning, foraging, resting at midday and foraging again before returning to one of their sleeping burrows at night. Neither searched systematically for the rest of the group and, as Flower and her party were in the eastern half of Whiskers' range while Badiel and the rest were in the west, the two halves did not meet for two weeks.

Eventually, the two parties met at a burrow in the western part of their range. Initially, they did not recognise each other and both began to war dance. They gradually approached and then, instead of attacking, mixed up, sniffing each other suspiciously. Flower moved around them, rubbing her chin against their faces and chattering. She growled warningly at her older daughters and bit Super Furry Animal at the base of the tail, then ignored her. Badiel initially avoided Flower and, when Flower eventually approached her, immediately grovelled and tried to groom her mother. But Flower was not to be placated and bit her on the base of the tail and on the neck and she turned and ran. Flower chased her out of the group and, though Badiel hung around for several days, she continued to keep her away. Badiel then disappeared and was not seen again.

Zaphod, too, was excited by the return of the missing animals. He scratched the ground, chinned the other males and rubbed his anal glands against anything within reach – including Flower and Super Furry Animal. Although he attacked Yossarian and forced him to submit, he made no attempt to drive him out. Yossarian made himself scarce and foraged well away from Flower and Zaphod on the edge of the group. In the burrow, he slept separately from the others and was usually the last animal to go below ground in the evening and the first up in the morning.

After the two halves of Whiskers rejoined one another, the group returned to its usual pattern of activity. With over thirty animals, they were now larger and stronger than all their neighbours. When they met Lazuli, they war danced and attacked and usually drove them away, pushing back the northern boundary of their range. One day, Whiskers foraged across the flats to the base of the Big Dune and then moved south across two dunes. Topping the third dune, they looked down to a grove of camel thorns growing beside the Big Dam. Two eland were browsing nearby, but the meerkats ignored them. There, at the burrow beside the dam, a sub-adult meerkat was sitting on her own. Flower's hair and tail went up and she started to war dance. The sub-adult saw her and quickly disappeared below ground. Flower and the rest of Whiskers bounded down to the burrow and sniffed at the entrance. Lazuli had clearly been busy here and it smelled as if there were pups underground. Flower led the way down, but had not gone far when the burrow walls narrowed and she came face to face with the sub-adult. Flower faced up to her opponent and tried to bite her and drag her back, but the sub-adult was quick and elusive and snapped back at her. Flower sparred with her for several minutes, but was reluctant to risk serious injury in an all-out attack and she eventually backed away and led the rest of the group back above ground.

* * *

It was now midsummer and the days were long and hot. Both Flower and Super Furry Animal were pregnant, while Mozart regularly attracted roving males from other groups and mated several times with one from Lazuli. Super Furry Animal was the first to give birth, but, the following evening, Flower led the group to another burrow to sleep. Super Furry Animal returned to the original burrow and successfully carried two of her pups to the new one, where the rest of the group were sleeping, but, the next evening, Flower led them all off to another sleeping burrow and Super Furry Animal finally abandoned her pups.

In mid-February 2005, Flower gave birth to her eighth litter of pups at the burrow below the Big Dune. This time the litter consisted of three females, Kim, Flo and Finn. Primed for breeding, Super Furry Animal began to lactate and helped her mother to suckle the new pups, who grew rapidly and began to forage with the group three weeks later. With so many to feed them, they quickly put on weight and rapidly became large and strong. After this litter, Flower became pregnant again, but had few reserves after producing and rearing her previous litter, and so aborted her new litter. Mozart was also pregnant and produced her pups in mid-March, but, this time, Flower killed and ate them. She had not yet fully regained condition after rearing her last litter and did not become pregnant again that season.

In March and April, heavy grey clouds blew in from the west and the sky was often overcast. It rained, and rained again, until the ground was sodden. Food was abundant and the meerkats lost little weight during the winter months, though they ceased to breed.

9

QUEEN OF THE DESERT

By mid-July 2005, Flower was pregnant again and becoming more and more aggressive, regularly attacking her older daughters. In the middle of August she evicted Mozart and, two days later, Super Furry Animal and her granddaughter, De La Soul. The three females repeatedly tried to rejoin the group, but Flower was not prepared to allow this and chased them out again each time, also evicting Kinkaju. In late August, Flower gave birth to her ninth litter, consisting of two males and two females. Two days later, she allowed the banished females to return and, once again, her pups all survived to forage with the group and grew rapidly after that.

The film teams returned in September. The first series of *Meerkat Manor* had been shown in America and was now being sold to other countries. Caroline planned another series, tracing the lives of Flower and her family through a second year.

After rearing her first litter of the season successfully, Flower produced and raised two further litters that summer, of five and three pups respectively. Each time, she evicted her older daughters from the group in the weeks before she gave birth. After giving birth to her first litter, she allowed them back, but after the second, she continued to chase them away. However, while the second of Flower's litters of pups were still in the burrow, Mozart managed to slip back and, after grovelling to Flower, was allowed to groom her. Mozart was heavily pregnant but, despite this, she was allowed to stay.

In the later stages of her pregnancy, Mozart became more and more aggressive to her sisters. She joined Flower in chasing away Kinkaju, Super Furry Animal and her niece, De La Soul, whenever they tried to re-enter the group. Finally, in late February 2006, she gave birth to two male pups and two females in the same burrow in which Flower's pups had been born. As before, Flower's pups remained there for longer than usual and the combined litter did not begin to forage with the group until Mozart's pups were three weeks old and Flower's were nearly six weeks old. Though Mozart's pups were still unusually small when the group left the breeding burrow, they all survived and grew rapidly once they were fed by the group members.

By the end of February, Flower was tired and thin from producing three litters, and regularly pilfered food from the others. With the help of Mozart she continued to keep her older daughters out of the group and they eventually left the study area. However, her ability to control her daughters was declining and the younger ones began to compete with each other for rank. Both Super Furry Animal and Armanita Ditch conceived; Super Furry Animal aborted her litter and Armanita Ditch produced hers early in March. Flower, who was pregnant again, immediately killed the pups and attacked Armanita Ditch. Cruise, who was now larger than her older sister, also attacked her and forced her out of the group. Armanita Ditch remained alone for a week and then rejoined the others and was viciously attacked once again. This time, she tolerated the beatings and was allowed to stay, but she was now clearly subordinate to her younger sister, Cruise, who bullied her mercilessly.

* * *

Throughout the season, Zaphod maintained his position as dominant male without difficulty. Yossarian remained in Whiskers, though he occasionally visited neighbouring groups in search of mating opportunities. Both were now seven years old. There were also nine males over a year old that had been born in the group: Flower's four-year-old nephew Big Will, her two-year-old sons, Stato and Pookie, her three yearling sons, Ragga Muffin, Pozzo and Zarathustra, and her three yearling grandsons, Flava Flav, Badboy Bubby and Arrested Development.

Yossarian, Big Will, Stato and Pookie were all regular rovers and sometimes the younger males went with them. Like Tarzan, they were often over-enthusiastic in pursuing females from neighbouring groups and sometimes paid a heavy price for this. A new group, Commandos, had formed to the east of the Whiskers range, involving some of the daughters of Risca, Flower's cousin, who had become the dominant female in Gattaca. Whiskers encountered them several times and there were battles, though Whiskers usually won. There were now a number of subordinate females in Commandos who had reached breeding age. Yossarian and Big Will visited them regularly, and, in late winter, led a large group of rovers from Whiskers on a visit to the group, including the yearling son of Badiel, Flava Flav, who was roving for the first time.

Again, like Tarzan, Flava Flav displayed more enthusiasm than cunning. He spotted a female on the edge of the group and darted in to sniff her without checking where the other members of Commandos group were. Unfortunately, one of the older males was just ten feet away, hidden by a tuft of grass, and, as soon as Flava appeared, he dashed out and grabbed him, biting at his back and neck. The other Commandos males ran out to join in the attack on Flava, who curled up to protect his stomach and face. The whole group then attempted to rip him apart while Flava cowered, screaming. The other Whiskers males watched from a safe distance, but made no attempt to intervene. After five minutes, the Commandos eventually lost interest, leaving Flava with a dislocated shoulder, large slashes to his legs and belly, a torn left eye socket and a ripped scrotum.

When they had finally gone, Flava staggered to his feet and dragged himself off towards Whiskers' range. On the way, he found an unused porcupine burrow where he was safe from eagles and ground predators. He spent the night there and did not emerge for the next two days. After this, he began to forage in the vicinity of the burrow and was able to find enough food to prevent himself from starving. Six days later, when Whiskers were grooming at their sleeping burrow before going for the night, he hobbled into the group and was reaccepted. Over the next three months, he made an astonishing recovery. His shoulder mended and he regained the use of his left eye. He even started to join his older brothers on roving trips again – though he was now much more circumspect in his courtship of strange females.

The older males continued to rove regularly, often visiting

Lazuli. Events among Whiskers' main rivals had taken an interesting turn. The dominant male, one of Zaphod's older brothers, had died, and potential immigrants had been kept out by the presence of several older males who had been born in the group and had not yet dispersed. As a result, Cazanna had no unrelated mating partners within Lazuli and she mated readily with outsiders. The Whiskers males all tried their luck with her and Yossarian and Zarathustra continued to go roving together.

With most of the older resident males off roving, Lazuli were left with only two yearling males. Yossarian and Zarathustra teamed up with a roving male from Young Ones and the three of them spent more and more time at Lazuli, mating with the dominant female and several of her daughters. They seldom returned to Whiskers at night and started to be accepted by the members of Lazuli. Unfortunately for them, one of the older Lazuli males left the Young Ones females that he had been consorting with and returned to Lazuli. He caught the intruders by surprise and immediately attacked them, and the rest of Lazuli joined in on his side. There was a vicious fight. Both Yossarian and the male from Young Ones were badly wounded and all three intruders were forced out of the group. Three days later, Zarathustra rejoined Whiskers, but Yossarian was not seen again.

* * *

After a year of unusually high rainfall, much of the study area was covered by a carpet of sourgrass. Food was abundant, but the long grass affected visibility and the meerkats were jumpy and nervous, spending as much of their time as possible in open areas where it had been flattened. To make matters worse, the grass flowered and produced a viscous juice that stuck to the meerkats' fur. When they groomed it off their ears, the skin came away too, so that many of them had raw edges to their ears. The long grass also affected our ability to collect regular data on the meerkats, and the observation schedules that we had carried out easily the previous year were now difficult to complete. When we followed the meerkats, we often ended up crashing through the grass, and regularly scared them. Also, with plenty of food available, they were less keen than usual to climb onto the scales to be weighed, so that obtaining regular records of their growth and condition became more of a problem. The grass also made it difficult for the camera crews to film the animals close up, or to follow them when they moved.

The grass died during the course of the summer, but was still tall and thick by the beginning of winter, and became a serious fire risk. We dreaded the electrical storms that flickered during the night. We practised fire drills and cut fire breaks around the houses and bought a large water container and a motor pump that could be mounted on the back of one of the pickup trucks to make a primitive fire engine.

Once again the winter was mild and, in August, Flower started evicting her daughters and older granddaughters. Though her granddaughter, De La Soul, was not yet two, she was one of the first to be chased away. Flower next evicted her oldest daughter, Mozart, and then her yearling daughters, Super Furry Animal, Kinkaju, Armanita Ditch and Monkulus. Super Furry Animal disappeared after this, while Monkulus returned to Whiskers. The Lazuli males found the remaining four more attractive than the Young Ones females and joined them to form a new group, which we called Starsky, and which defended a territory to the south-west of the Whiskers range. Though Mozart was the oldest by some distance, Kinkaju, her younger sister, took dominance.

Over the past year, Whiskers had secured their position as

the largest and most successful group in the study area, and continued to extend their range. They took the whole of the Big Dune and all the ground between it and the Big Dam from Lazuli. To the east they pushed back Vivian and to the west they forced Elveera to abandon their closest sleeping burrow. To the south they drove Young Ones back nearly to the road and encountered the new group, Commandos, that had formed to the south-east of their range. They attacked them immediately and severely wounded the dominant male. After this, Commandos moved its range further to the east.

In early September Flower produced three pups. None of the other females in the group were pregnant and the pups survived. This litter was Flower's twelfth; she had now raised forty-five pups in all. One of the unusual characteristics of co-operative breeders, where the offspring of dominant females are raised by other group members, is that breeding females can have large litters at short intervals and commonly have long lifespans. The most successful female meerkat we have monitored, the dominant female of the group called Drie Doring, maintained her position for ten years and gave birth to eighty-five surviving pups. Dominant female naked mole-rats and termite queens can live for over twenty years, popping out eggs or babies at a prodigious rate, and so can have a remarkable number of offspring. In theory, dominant female naked mole-rats can bear over several hundred offspring in their lives, while termite queens may produce many thousands. However, the long tenure of dominant females means that very few females ever acquire top status. Most are evicted from the group where they have hatched or been born and, unless they can establish a new breeding group, probably die within a few months. Our estimates suggest that between eighty and ninety per cent of all female meerkats never breed as dominants and most die before the age of three. As a result, competition between females for breeding positions is intense, and females have evolved hormonal and physical adaptations that enhance their competitive ability.

The tenure of dominant male meerkats is only around half that of females, perhaps partly because they are more likely than dominant females to be displaced by animals from other groups, and partly because, unlike dominant females, they typically disperse if their partner dies. This means that a higher proportion of male meerkats are likely to breed as dominants, so competition between males, though strong, is not as intense as among females.

* * *

While Flower's twelfth litter of pups were still at the burrow where they had been born, I spent two weeks with Whiskers before flying back to England. On the last day, I went to their breeding burrow to take photographs of all the surviving members of the group. They were using one of their regular breeding burrows on the side of a spur of dunes sticking out onto the South Flats. Arriving at the burrow before the group got up, I watched the daily events of the Kalahari unfolding: a group of springbok that had moved onto the flats in the night starting to drift back to the dunes as the light grew; two hartebeest stepping carefully up the slope of the dunes; a pair of crowned plovers displaying noisily at their neighbours, flapping lazily across the flats in conspicuous displays; compact groups of social weavers flying past, off to distant foraging grounds. As the sun rose and the air warmed, lilac-breasted rollers began to display. High above the flats, groups of sandgrouse flew out to distant feeding grounds, calling to each other. On all sides the green-grey scrub stretched to the horizon, edged on the east by the blue line of the Koranaberg Hills.

I reflected on our work over the last fourteen years. When you watch animals without being able to recognise individuals, you commonly see stability – birds nesting in the same box each year, bull elk rutting in the same stand. This often leads people to assume that animals are much older than they really are: in Scotland, I had met a deer stalker who recognised the same red deer stag rutting at the same site for twenty years. In practice, he had probably seen four or five different stags rutting at the same site in successive years. When you are able to recognise individuals with certainty, as we can, you start to see how quickly individuals pass through their lifespans, how fast the tides of life flow. In meerkats most individuals are probably dead before their third birthday, even dominant breeders seldom live for more than ten years.

Meerkats are clearly one of the most co-operative of all mammals and the readiness of subordinates to assist with rearing the offspring of dominant breeders is remarkable. There is no evidence that individuals are forced to contribute to co-operative activities or that they attempt to avoid doing so, though they do less work when they are hungry or in poor condition. Generous animals commonly appear to be more anxious than other group members, less occupied with finding food, more easily distracted by the possibility of danger to themselves and others. When they are on guard or babysitting, they give the strong impression that they are intent on what they are doing. If we offer food to guards or babysitters, generally they are not interested. Our research on hormonal mechanisms confirms that variation in co-operative behaviour is affected by physiological changes.

Most group members are close relatives – their average degree of relatedness is around the level of a half-brother, so that helpers get important indirect benefits through assisting kin. However, they do not aid close relatives more than other group members,

Playing yearlings practise fighting techniques.

Pups that get left behind are obviously agitated and call loudly.

Left Following the death of a dominant female, several subordinates conceive litters.

Above To keep warm on winter mornings, pups huddle in the shelter of their babysitters. Sometimes only their noses are visible.

Above An adult male on guard on a fallen tree. Guards give a regular call – known as the 'watchman's song' – that lets other group members know that there is a sentinel on duty.

Opposite page

Above left A shared view. Pups learn much about their environment from babysitters.

Left Pups threatened by a predator bunch with hair and tail erect, just as adults do.

Left Pups watch babysitters closely and learn from their reactions.

Below left When it is cold, pups use babysitters for shelter and warmth.

Below Pups emerge from the burrow when they are around two weeks old. When the group leaves each day, one adult remains behind to babysit.

After scenting or hearing their prey, meerkats dig rapidly through the loose sand, often shifting several times their own weight.

Sometimes they disappear into the hole they are digging and can no longer keep a watch for danger.

Whiskers mobbing a Cape cobra. Meerkats frequently mob larger snakes, but seldom attack them directly.

Flower at six years old.

and immigrant males, who are unrelated to most other individuals, usually do as much work as anyone else, suggesting that helping must provide other advantages too. As our study progressed, it became increasingly clear what these were likely to be. In small groups, individuals are more prone to be attacked and killed by predators, they have to work harder to raise pups, their territory is more likely to be taken over by their neighbours and their chances of successfully dispersing and establishing themselves as breeders elsewhere are much reduced. It pays everyone to do their best to help raise recruits in order to maintain the size of their group.

This still does not explain why individuals make no obvious attempt to cheat or free-ride on the system. Why do they not allow the other members of the group to do their share of the work? There are two likely reasons for this. First, the costs of helping are not high in terms of survival and breeding success, since contributions to co-operative activities are adjusted to the individual's body condition. Generous helpers, for example, are no more likely to die or be killed than less generous ones. Second, shirking can affect the survival and breeding success of kin, so the indirect benefits of co-operation probably play a role. An individual that failed to help protect other group members or rear additional pups would be risking the future survival and breeding success of its relatives, as well as its own chances of surviving and breeding. It is in everyone's interest to keep the size of the group large, as it is to defend the group's territory against invaders. They are all in it together. No meerkat is an island.

Since only a small number of animals breed effectively, there is intense competition between group members for the dominant position. This is usually suppressed, for there are risks to subordinates in attacking dominant individuals as this can lead to eviction from the group. However, when a dominant female dies, the adult females in the group fight for her position. It is not difficult to see why, for their chances of surviving are low if they do not acquire dominant status within their first three years, and the potential reproductive pay-offs of acquiring the breeding position are very large. The intensity of female competition is closely associated with the degree of co-operation, for it is precisely because breeding females require assistance from helpers to breed that dominant females prevent subordinates from breeding.

Competition between dominant and subordinate females is also intense. Dominant females do their best to limit the growth of subordinate females and to evict larger or older animals before they are in a position to challenge them, especially if they are not close relatives. While subordinates are still in the group, the dominant female tries to prevent them from breeding to minimise the risk that her own pups will be killed by pregnant subordinates or that other pups will compete with her own offspring. Since reproductive suppression, infanticide and eviction limit group size, there are costs involved – but they are outweighed by the benefits of securing her own reproductive success. The result is continuous competition between dominant females and subordinates, which is usually won by the dominant. However, in the early years of their tenure, when they are not much older or heavier than subordinates, dominant females are insecure; subordinates often breed and may also challenge them for their position. In addition, towards the end of their lives, the dominants' physical condition declines, they commonly lose the ability to control subordinates, and their reproductive success falls. Subordinates are unforgiving and will readily evict their mothers or sisters if they get an opportunity to do so. Males, too, compete intensely for dominant position, and, like females, they are opportunistic in their challenges, commonly waiting until a competitor is ill or exhausted after a fight or a breeding attempt before attacking them. No holds are barred.

The recognition that social relations between group members involve conflict as well as co-operation has important implications for our view of animal societies. In the past, the tendency has been to see groups of co-operative vertebrates as tug-of-war teams made up of individuals with a common interest that are pulling together to produce and rear babies. But the interests of group members are rarely identical and conflicts between them generate intense competition within groups.

The infanticidal behaviour of female meerkats provides a good example. It is in the interests of subordinate females to breed when they can, and in those of dominants to do their best to stop them when this endangers the survival of their own offspring. Sometimes subordinates manage to breed, sometimes they don't – but the struggle leads to the production and loss of substantial numbers of pups and it would not be difficult to design a more efficient system. However, the struggle persists because the interests of breeders and helpers differ and both are trying to extract maximum benefits from the system.

Most vertebrate societies resemble human soap operas more closely than tug-of-war teams. Group members share some interests and co-operation is common, but individuals are also pursuing their own objectives, often at a cost to other group members. The strong rarely go out of their way to protect the interests of the weak unless they are close relatives, mates or regular allies, and individuals that kill other group members are neither evicted nor shunned.

The specialised co-operative societies of bees, wasps and ants are much more similar to tug-of-war teams than those of vertebrates.

In many social insects, group members are more closely related to each other than they are in vertebrates, so that conflicts of interest are reduced. Workers are often unable to breed, which means that their only chance of propagating their genes is by assisting related breeders. Even here, the interests of different individuals are not identical, but the potential for conflict is greatly reduced. It is not unreasonable to regard the colonies of some social insects as super-organisms.

So what about humans and other primates? In most non-human primates, crafty competition, rather than extensive co-operation, is the order of the day. In many social primates, relatives or allies support each other in competitive interactions with other families or alliances. However, all adult females breed regularly and group members rarely suckle or feed each other's offspring or collectively attack predators. The most co-operative of the primates are the marmosets and tamarins of South America, where a single female breeds in each group and other group members help to carry and care for her offspring – but even these species do not show the level of co-operation found in meerkats and mole-rats.

Patterns of human reproduction resemble those of other primates rather than those of specialised co-operative breeders. Most adult females breed and, although women may synchronise their reproductive cycles, they do not commonly suppress each other's fertility. However, there is one important aspect of their life cycle in which women differ from other primates. In all human populations, women cease to be fertile between the age of fifty and sixty, several years before the end of their lives. In many societies, grandmothers play an important role in raising their grand-children, and, in some cases, children whose grandmothers are still alive have a better chance of surviving than those whose grandmothers have died. There are several different explanations of the evolution of the menopause in humans, but one is that it evolved because women of over fifty or so could increase the number of their descendants more effectively by helping to look after their daughters' children than by attempting to breed themselves.

While humans may not be specialised co-operative breeders like meerkats or mole-rats, their co-operative behaviour shows a level of development and sophistication that is absent in other animals. Collective exploration and production of resources, including hunting, fishing and cultivation, are widespread. Like many other social animals, humans also co-operate to defend themselves and their resources against neighbouring communities. But in human societies, unrelated individuals commonly assist each other, often forming teams where individuals who make different but complementary contributions to co-ordinated activities share the benefits. Goods and services are commonly exchanged and group members co-operate to enforce behavioural norms by punishing antisocial behaviour, such as rape, murder and (in some cases) theft, often at a cost to themselves.

So why do humans co-operate so widely with unrelated individuals? Unsurprisingly, there is little consensus on the answer, and studies of animals are of limited relevance. They do, however, provide some signposts. In the relatively small groups of Pleistocene hominids, levels of kinship between group members were probably reasonably high, as they are still in many tribal human societies, so that individuals who assisted other group members were, on average, likely to be contributing to the survival and breeding success of their relatives. As with many other co-operative animals, members of large groups were probably able to exploit resources, defend themselves against predators and neighbours and raise offspring more effectively than members of small groups. Defence against aggressors was probably of particular importance in encouraging co-operation, and remains so today. In the Yanomamo indians of Venezuela, neighbouring villages used, until recently, to raid each other, stealing food and women. Who won? The larger villages. And who usually wins when countries fight each other? Usually (though not invariably) the larger, richer country.

But humans frequently act together in ways that do not contribute to the success of their community and neither kin-selected benefits nor the benefits of group size explain the complexity of their collaboration. So what is it about humans that has allowed co-operation between unrelated individuals, as well as between relatives, to reach such levels? The answer is probably language. With language, individuals can make agreements to provide reciprocal assistance or to share resources. With language, group members can decide on customs or rules, can agree penalties for failing to reciprocate, and can enforce them. Without language, animals cannot make explicit agreements to assist each other and are locked into a system where individuals pursue their immediate interests. Humans have the ability to transcend these limitations.

*   *   *

As the light strengthened, the first face appeared at the entrance to the main burrow. It was Flava Flav, Flower's two-year-old nephew. One by one the other members of the group emerged. I moved around them, taking a portrait of each animal in turn. Flower's oldest daughter, Rocket Dog, now almost three, and her younger sisters, Monkulus, Hawkeye, Cruise and Tina Sparkle, Mozart's two year old daughter; Flower's six yearling daughters and her five daughters that were less than a year old. In addition, there were nineteen males. At seven years old, Zaphod, Flower's partner, was the oldest by more than five years. There were Flower's four two-year-old sons, Pozzo and Zarathustra and Logan and Mitch. and her four two-year-old grandsons, the offspring of Mozart and Badiel. In addition, there were Flower's four yearling sons, and, below them, six male juveniles. Thirty-seven animals in all. The largest number Whiskers had ever reached and the biggest and most successful group in the population we had been studying.

Gradually the animals began to feed and spread out. As usual, Flower was keen to move off, and a bunch of meerkats started to form below the breeding burrow. Flava set off down a well-marked game track, and Rocket Dog and Logan went after him. Flower made up her mind and, followed by Zaphod, she headed off down the same path with the rest of the group in line behind her. Only Rocket Dog stayed behind to guard the pups. I made for home to pack up.

EPILOGUE

I did not see Flower again. The last quarter of 2006 was unusually arid and food was scarce. Much of Whiskers' range was a tangle of dry grass that made foraging difficult and visibility poor. Whiskers left the northern parts of their range, and moved down onto the South Flats, displacing Young Ones to the south. Flower had successfully raised her twelfth litter of pups and produced another litter, her thirteenth, in late November. She was in poor condition and there were only two pups, one of whom had a deformed leg. Halfway through the period of babysitting, Flower's milk began to dry up and the pups had to be nursed by two of her yearling daughters.

The film crew returned to shoot the third series of *Meerkat Manor* programmes. The grass continued to make their lives difficult, but was not as bad as it had been the previous year. Whiskers was still so large that it was often difficult for all members of the group to remain in contact with each other. Early in 2007, the two halves of Whiskers became separated. Flower led one half, including Zaphod, back towards the Big Dam in the western part of their range, abandoning her two pups at the breeding burrow. Twenty-three members of the group, including her two-year-old daughter Rocket Dog, who was pregnant, her two sons, Zarathustra and Pozzo, and her grandson, Flava Flav, remained on the South Flats and continued to sleep at the breeding burrow. Flower's pups were nursed by her yearling daughters and survived to forage with the group, but were weak and were abandoned two days later, while the group was foraging. Soon afterwards, Rocket Dog gave birth to one premature pup above ground, and her yearling brother, Machu Picchu, ate it.

The two halves of Whiskers remained apart for nearly a month and Rocket Dog took over the role of dominant female in her half. All the males were close relatives of the group's females, and no clear dominant male emerged. Over the course of the month, Young Ones made several attempts to return to the South Flats and eventually encountered the half of Whiskers that had remained. Like Whiskers, they had been affected by the drought and had one rather underdeveloped pup with them, the last survivor of a litter of five. Even though only half of Whiskers had remained on the South Flats, they were able to put Young Ones to flight and regularly did so. In the course of one fight, the Young Ones' pup was separated from its group and became mixed up with Whiskers. Whiskers did not recognise it as belonging to their neighbours and took it with them when they left. With so many willing feeders, the pup was quickly stuffed full of food and grew rapidly. It never returned to its original group.

At the turn of the year, the rains eventually arrived, insect populations increased and the meerkats' condition improved. Both Flower and Rocket Dog became pregnant again, but the ability of both females to suppress the other females in their groups was weak and many of them conceived, too. In early January 2007, Flower led her animals back east to the South Flats and the two factions of Whiskers eventually met. They briefly war danced at each other, then mixed but did not fight. Flower and Zaphod sniffed the other members of the group carefully, then relaxed and the two halves mingled. Flower immediately assumed dominance of them all and there was no challenge from Rocket Dog.

On 25 January Whiskers got up as usual and sunned. They had been using their favourite burrow in the Eastern Thickets. It had rained in the night and the sand was wet and sticky. They set off as usual, moving south-west, and foraged in the small valleys behind the dunes on the north edge of the South Flats. At midday, they rested around the bole of a large shepherd's tree on the crest of the dunes and, when the heat had begun to fade, foraged along the dune crest overlooking the South Flats. As the sun fell and began to cast long shadows, Flower led them down to the burrow on the flank of the dune where she had given birth to her previous litter. At a nearby burrow, three ground squirrels were feeding, but the main entrance to the burrow had not been disturbed. Flower carefully scrutinised the burrow from a distance and, followed by the rest of her group, walked up to the main entrance. She sniffed at it cautiously and inspected each of the other burrows before she went in.

As Flower entered the burrow she was aware of an unusual smell. She stopped and listened but there was no sound. She moved further underground, treading carefully, while her family followed. After a day in the open, her eyes adapted gradually to the darkness and she did not see the broad, smooth slick on the sand in front of her. She went on, her senses alert, while her family pressed behind.

Suddenly, there was a movement. Flower backed away, but the tunnel behind her was narrow and her family pressed close. In a side burrow, there was a large snake, which struck at her. The first time it missed, but on its second strike it caught Flower's head between its jaws, delivering a full dose of poison. The snake coiled back and waited while Flower stood, dazed and in pain. She backed up the slope into the daylight and stood rocking on her feet. Her family ignored her. The sun was now below the horizon and it was getting cool. The animals avoided the burrow where Flower had been attacked and drifted across to a satellite burrow fifty yards away, unconnected to the main one. Flower stumbled after them and went below to sleep.

At dawn the next day, the group began to emerge. Flower's oldest daughter, Rocket Dog, was the first up, followed by Zaphod and all the rest of Flower's offspring and grandchildren. They turned to face the rising sun, or began to groom themselves. However, they were restless and ill at ease, and kept glancing at the burrow.

Eventually, Flower appeared at the entrance, rocking from side to side. Her head and jaw were swollen and one eye was half shut. She stumbled to one side of the burrow and lay, breathing heavily. She had aborted during the night and there was some blood on her rear. Zaphod came across to her and groomed her briefly.

As the sun mounted, the rest of Flower's family stopped sunning and started to feed. They were uneasy and called regularly. Eventually, Rocket Dog led them off to the south and one by one they followed her. Flower tried to follow but fell and crawled back to the burrow entrance, where she lay in the shadow. As Zaphod left, he marked Flower on the head.

The sun climbed and the heat of the day rose and the effects of the large dose of poison that Flower had received became stronger. Her breathing grew laboured and then lighter and lighter as she lost consciousness. By the afternoon she was in a coma, though she still twitched occasionally. Flies had started to gather on her face. Her breathing became shallower and shallower and finally ceased.

*   *   *

Flower's death ended a remarkable life story. She was approaching her seventh birthday when she died and had been the dominant female of Whiskers for five years. All thirty-seven members of the group apart from Zaphod were either her children or her grandchildren. Flowers's obvious successor, Rocket Dog, was her daughter and two of her evicted daughters, Kinkaju and Mozart, were the oldest females in the new breeding group that had formed to the east of Whiskers' range. In the months following Flower's death, Whiskers again became split and, this time, the two halves remained separate – one led by Rocket Dog and one by Monkulus. Several of Flower's sons and daughters had emigrated out of the study area and must either have died or established themselves as breeders in other groups. She also had many other relatives still living in our study population. Her first cousin, Risca, had emigrated with Izit to form Gattaca and most of that group were her cousins. Holly's mother, her grandmother, had been the dominant female of Young Ones for over eight years, so most members of Young Ones were related to her in some way.

Within a few days of Flower's death, her six daughters gave birth to their litters and the group began to babysit. Eventually, a combined litter emerged, including the offspring of several of Flower's daughters. All the adult females in the group had been born since Zaphod had joined them and refused to breed with him, so Zaphod's reproductive opportunities were limited. For the first time since he had become the dominant male, he contributed to babysitting, and, when the pups grew and began to forage with the group, he turned into one of the most assiduous helpers. As yet, he has not begun to visit other groups, but he will probably start to prospect for new breeding opportunities as the year progresses – he is unlikely to stay in Whiskers for long.

We have come a long way since the early days when we struggled to follow a single group and had difficulty recognising individuals. We now work with fourteen different groups, which range in size from around a dozen animals to the thirty-seven of Whiskers. All three hundred members of these groups are individually identifiable and we have followed the lives of almost all of them from the time they emerged, blinking in the bright sunlight as three-week-old pups. We know their ages precisely and have been able to measure their growth and development. We know who their mothers are, and, in many cases, their fathers too. We know which individuals are littermates and how individuals are related to the other members of their group. As breeding females progress through their careers we can measure their breeding success and, when they die, we are usually able to identify the cause of death. Our ability to recognise and monitor individuals has allowed us to answer a range of questions not previously investigated in co-operative mammals and has generated more than sixty scientific papers. But there is still much that we don't understand. Just how do dominant females control reproduction by other females? Why do dominant females sometimes prevent evicted females from returning to the group and sometimes allow them to do so? To what extent can dominant females control the co-operative behaviour of other group members? The life histories of Flower and her offspring and of all the other individuals in the population will eventually provide the answers. Our work goes on.

Tim Clutton-Brock

1 May 2007

CHRONOLOGY OF FLOWER'S LIFE

WHISKERS AT FLOWER'S BIRTH 15/03/2000

At Flower's birth, Whiskers consists of nineteen animals. Females include her mother (and the dominant female of the group) Holly (VYF008, b. 09/12/96); her cousins Risca (VWF004, b. 17/08/98), Aphrodite (VWF009, b. 28/11/98), Artemis (VWF610, b. 28/11/98) and her sisters Zola (VWF011, b. 14/07/99), Vialli (VWF012, b. 14/07/99), Aramis (VWF016, b. 31/01/99) and Wahine (VWF019, b. 21/12/99). Males include the dominant male, Argon (VLM002, b. 10/03/96), his brother Delpheus (VLM003, b. 10/03/96), a previously unknown immigrant called Beetle (VWM001, b. circa 01/01/98), Flower's cousins Lancelot (VWM007, b. 28/11/98), Jean-Luc (VWM008, b. 28/11/98) and her brothers Dennis Wise (VWM014, b. 14/07/99), Athos (VWM015, b. 03/10/99), Porthos (VWM018, b. 03/10/99), Tama (VWM020, b. 21/12/99), Rangi (VWM021, b. 21/12/99) and Orgali (VMM012, b. 21/12/99).

EVENTS

15/03/2000   Holly, the dominant female of Whiskers, gives birth to Flower (VWF026), Petal (VWF023), Thumper (VWM025) and Hazel (VWM024).

07/04/2000   Petal is killed.

03/09/2000   Holly evicts her nieces Risca, Aphrodite and Artemis.

08/09/2000	Holly gives birth to three pups, Mr Burns (VWM028), Smithers (VWF029), and VWP027.
19/09/2000	Holly is killed. Risca assumes dominance.
22/09/2000	Aphrodite and Artemis return to the group.
25/09/2000	VWP027 dies.
28/09/2000	Artemis gives birth to two pups, VWM030 and Ugly Pup (VWF031).
06/10/2000	Delpheus leaves the group as he cannot breed with any of the females. Since Holly's death, all the females in the group are related to him.
22/10/2000	Argon leaves the group as, like Delpheus, he is now related to all the females and so cannot breed.
01/11/2000	Ugly Pup (VWF031) is savaged by Young Ones but survives.
10/11/2000	Following the death of Holly, Risca, Aphrodite, Artemis, Zola, Aramis and Vialli all become pregnant.
15/11/2000	Risca evicts Artemis and Aphrodite.
20/11/2001	Beetle establishes himself as dominant male.
18/12/2000	Risca gives birth. Her litter is killed by Aphrodite.
24/12/2000	Zola gives birth. Her litter is killed by Artemis.
26/12/2000	Vialli gives birth. Her litter is killed by Artemis.
12/01/2001	Aphrodite, Aramis and Wahine give birth. Their litters are killed by Artemis, who is the last remaining pregnant female.
19/01/2001	Artemis gives birth to Rydapuni (VWF034), Dangerous Dave (VWM035) and Mi Julie (VWF036). Her litter is suckled by her sisters whose litters she had killed.
24/05/2001	Risca evicts Aphrodite and Artemis.
12/06/2001	Zola and Aramis are evicted.
26/06/2001	The Whiskers males (VWM001, VWM007, VWM014, VWM018, VWM020, VWM021, VWM022, VWM024, VWM025, VWM028) leave the group to go roving.

27/06/2001	A large coalition of Vivian males occupies the group – including Izit (VVM021), Basil (VVM015), Zaphod (VVM032), Yossarian (VVM033), Genghis (VVM035), Alexander (VVM037), Govinda (VVM041) and Phooey (VVM046). Risca mates with them. Izit assumes dominance.
27/07/2001	Attila (VVM036) and Patis (VVM058) join Whiskers from Vivian.
28/07/2001	Zazu (VVM027) joins Whiskers from Vivian.
14/08/2001	Risca gives birth. Her litter dies before emerging from the burrow.
09/08/2001	Basil emigrates, joins up with other Vivian males and immigrates into Lazuli.
30/08/2001	Izit loses dominance. The Vivian males compete for his position.
05/09/2001	Older Vivian males go roving. Zazu returns first and assumes dominance.
24/09/2001	Risca loses dominance. Wahine and Flower compete for her position.
22/09/2001	Zazu is deposed. The Vivian males compete for dominance.
23/09/2001	Vialli and Zaphod assume dominance. Risca is evicted.
30/09/2001	Izit and Genghis emigrate.
11/10/2001	Zazu emigrates and joins Lazuli.
17/10/2001	Govinda emigrates and joins Lazuli.
05/11/2001	Risca and Wahine join up with Izit, Vervain (VVM049) and DeeJay (VVM063) to form Gattaca.
01/11/2001	Vialli and Flower are both pregnant.
19/11/2001	Flower gives birth. Her litter is killed by Vialli.
21/11/2001	Flower is evicted by Vialli.
22/11/2001	Vialli gives birth to Big Will (VWM038), Itchy (VWF039), Scratchy (VWF040), Thelma (VWF041), Louise (VWF042), Daisy (VWF043) and Tarzan (VWM044).
25/11/2001	Flower returns to the group.
06/12/2001	Ugly Pup gives birth. Her litter dies.
24/01/2002	Vialli is killed.

07/02/2002   Flower assumes dominance.

07/02/2002   Flower, Smithers and Mi Julie are all pregnant.

26/02/2002   Flower gives birth. Her litter is killed.

14/03/2002   Mi Julie gives birth. Her litter is killed by Smithers.

17/03/2002   Smithers gives birth. Her litter is killed.

22/03/2002   Ugly Pup gives birth to three pups (VWM046, VWP047, VWP048).

23/04/2002   Whiskers and Lazuli fight. Lazuli kill VWP047.

15/06/2002   VWM046 is killed by a predator.

09/07/2002   Flower is pregnant.

14/07/2002   Mi Julie and Ugly Pup are evicted by Flower.

16/07/2002   Smithers and Rydapuni are evicted by Flower.

18/08/2002   Flower gives birth to her first surviving litter: Badiel (VWF049, alias Tosca), Stato (VWM050) and Skinner (VWF051).

07/10/2002   Flower is pregnant.

08/11/2002   Flower gives birth to her second litter, fathered by Zaphod. It includes Einstein (VWM052), Mozart (VWF053), Shakespeare (VWM054) and Freud (VWM055).

17/01/2003   Flower is pregnant.

22/01/2003   Itchy gives birth. Her litter is killed.

24/01/2003   Flower gives birth to her third litter: Pookie (VWM057), VWM056 and VWF058.

12/02/2003   Alexander fights Zaphod and loses. Yossarian attacks Zaphod and loses. Phooey attacks Zaphod and loses. Yossarian attacks Zaphod again and eventually wins.

13/02/2003   Yossarian assumes dominance. He regularly attacks other males.

01/03/2003   Scratchy gives birth. Her pups are later abandoned.

06/03/2003   VWF058 is killed.

07/03/2003   Alexander and Dangerous Dave attack Zaphod and evict him.

18/03/2003   Freud disappears.

21/03/2003	VWM056 dies.
23/03/2003	Thelma gives birth. Her pups are abandoned.
29/05/2003	Dangerous Dave leaves the group.
07/08/2003	Flower is pregnant.
12/09/2003	Flower aborts her litter.
19/09/2003	Tarzan visits Young Ones and is attacked and seriously wounded.
06/10/2003	Scratchy is pregnant.
16/10/2003	Flower is pregnant. She evicts Scratchy and Louise.
19/10/2003	Phooey attacks Yossarian and loses.
21/10/2003	Flower evicts Itchy, Thelma and Daisy.
28/10/2003	Scratchy gives birth. Flower finds her burrow and evicts the babysitter. The group remains at the burrow but Scratchy is not allowed to rejoin the group. Scratchy returns to the burrow to suckle her pups when Whiskers are absent. The pups eventually die.
28/10/2003	Itchy, Scratchy and Daisy are seen for the last time.
14/11/2003	Louise is evicted by Flower and not seen again.
06/12/2003	Flower gives birth to her fourth litter: Kinkaju (VWF059), Rocket Dog (VWF060), Raga Muffin (VWM061) and Super Furry Animal (VWF062). Badiel and Mozart are allocated to look after them.
21/12/2003	Mozart aborts.
16/01/2004	Flower is pregnant.
19/01/2004	Badiel is pregnant.
22/02/2004	Flower gives birth to her fifth litter: Monkulus (VWF063), Armanita Ditch (VWF064), Pozzo (VWM065), Lucky (VWF066) and Zarathustra (VWM067).
27/02/2004	Mozart is pregnant.
09/03/2004	Badiel gives birth to her litter: De La Soul (VWF068), Arrested Development (VWM069), Flava Flav (VWM070) and Bad Boy Bubby (VWM071).
26/03/2004	Mozart gives birth. Her litter is abandoned.

17/04/2004	Mozart is pregnant again.
22/04/2004	Flower is pregnant.
27/04/2004	Alexander attacks Yossarian and loses. Soon after, Zaphod attacks Yossarian and wins, attaining dominance.
12/05/04	Flower and Mozart both abort.
07/06/2004	Lucky is killed.
11/06/2004	Flower is pregnant.
19/07/2004	Flower aborts.
08/08/2004	Flower, Mozart and Badiel are all pregnant. Flower fails to evict her daughters.
06/09/2004	Flower gives birth to her sixth litter: Hawkeye (VWF062), Logan (VWM073), Mitch (VWM074) and Cruise (VWF075).
28/09/2004	Mozart gives birth to Tina Sparkle (VWF076), VWF077, VWM078 and VWM079.
10/10/2004	Badiel gives birth to Maladoy (VWM080), Jogu (VWM081) and VWM082.
10/10/2004	Einstein and Alexander leave the group.
18/10/2004	Yossarian moves Flower's pups to another burrow. Badiel transfers her pups and so does Mozart, though VWP079 is abandoned.
02/10/2004	VWP082 and VWF077 disappear.
17/11/2004	Flower evicts Mozart.
22/11/2004	Flower evicts Badiel.
23/11/2004	Shakespeare is bitten by a puff adder.
06/12/2004	Flower (VWF026) gives birth to her seventh litter: Petra (VWF082), Machu Picchu (VWM084), Ningaloo (NWM085) and Popkat (VWP086).
08/12/2004	Mozart rejoins the group.
03/01/2005	The group split. Popkat disappears. Super Furry Animal assumes dominance in the splinter group. Badiel rejoins the group and takes control from Super Furry Animal.
17/01/2005	The group reunites. Flower evicts Badiel, who later disappears.

21/01/2005	Flower is pregnant.
28/01/2005	Super Furry Animal gives birth. Her pups initially survive but are later abandoned.
22/02/2005	Flower gives birth to her eighth litter: Kim (VWM089), Flo (VWF090) and Finn (VWF091).
02/03/2005	Mozart is pregnant.
11/03/2005	Shakespeare disappears.
25/03/2005	Flower is pregnant.
01/04/2005	Flower aborts her litter.
16/04/2005	Mozart gives birth. Her pups are killed by Flower.
07/05/2005	Ragga Muffin disappears.
20/06/2005	Whiskers males visit Commandos. Flava Flav is caught and attacked.
14/07/2005	Flower is pregnant.
17/08/2005	Flower evicts Mozart.
19/08/2005	Super Furry Animal and De La Soul are evicted.
24/08/2005	Flower evicts Kinkaju.
26/08/2005	Flower gives birth to her ninth litter of pups: Billy (VWF093), Miles (VWM094), Ella (VWF095) and Baker (VWM096).
26/08/2005	All the evicted females return.
10/09/2005	Whiskers splits in half.
07/10/2005	Yossarian goes roving and mates with Pancake (VLF092) from Lazuli.
12/10/2005	Flower is pregnant.
04/11/2005	Flower evicts Mozart and De La Soul.
05/11/2005	Super Furry Animal is evicted.
11/11/2005	Flower gives birth to her tenth litter, which contains five pups: Bananas (VWF097), Butch Cassidy (VWM098), Sundance (VWF099), Alonzo Mourning (VWM100) and Orinoco (VWM101).
15/11/2005	Mozart, Kinkaju, Super Furry Animal and De La Soul return to the group.

07/12/2005	Kinkaju and Armanita Ditch are pregnant.
28/12/2005	Kinkaju and Armanita Ditch abort.
02/01/2006	Flower is pregnant.
02/01/2006	Sundance disappears.
15/01/2006	Mozart is pregnant.
22/01/2006	Flower evicts Mozart and Super Furry Animal.
23/01/2006	Flower evicts De La Soul.
23/01/2006	Big Will, Stato, Pookie, Arrested Development and Bad Boy Bubby leave the group.
24/01/2006	Flower evicts Kinkaju.
29/01/2006	Flower gives birth to her eleventh litter: Panthro (VWM012), Cheetara (VWF013) and Wiley Kat (VWF014).
06/02/2006	Mozart, still pregnant, rejoins the group. Mozart assists Flower in keeping her sisters out of the group.
24/02/2006	Mozart gives birth to Wollow (VWM105), Lilly the Pink (VWF016), Ju Drop (VWF017) and Karim (VWM018).
02/03/2006	Flower, Super Furry Animal and Armanita Ditch are all pregnant.
02/03/2006	Super Furry Animal aborts.
03/04/2006	Armanita Ditch gives birth. Her pups are killed.
06/04/2006	Armanita Ditch is evicted from the group by her sister, Cruise.
07/04/2006	Flower aborts her litter.
12/04/2006	Armanita Ditch returns to the group.
01/07/2006	Flower is pregnant.
04/07/2006	Yossarian leaves Whiskers with Zarathustra and approaches Lazuli, whose males have left the group.
10/07/2006	Returning Lazuli males attack Yossarian, killing one of his allies.
13/07/2006	Zarathustra returns to Whiskers. Yossarian disappears.
25/07/2006	Flower evicts Mozart, Kinkaju and De La Soul.
29/07/2006	Flower evicts Super Furry Animal and Armanita Ditch.

24/08/2006	Flower evicts Monkulus.
25/08/2006	The evicted Whiskers females are joined by two Lazuli males and form new group, Starsky. Kinkaju assumes dominance.
02/09/2006	Flower gives birth to her twelfth litter: Suggs (VWM109), Izzy (VWF110) and Busta (VWM111).
21/09/2006	Kim is killed by a vehicle.
01/10/2006	The dry period begins. It will continue until 01/03/2007. Whiskers move onto the South Flats.
20/11/2006	Flower (VWF026) gives birth to her thirteenth litter: two very small pups.
03/12/2006	Whiskers splits. Flower's pups remain with the other half of the group and are suckled by Finn and Bananas. Rocket Dog takes dominance in the other half of Whiskers.
14/12/2006	Rocket Dog aborts.
19/12/2006	Flower's pups disappear soon after they begin to forage with the group.
23/12/2006	A Young Ones pup (VYM137) is mixed up in the mêlée following an intergroup fight and remains with Whiskers.
26/12/2006	The two halves of Whiskers reunite. Flower retakes overall dominance.
27/12/2006	Eight Whiskers females are pregnant, including Flower.
25/01/2007	Flower is bitten by a snake and dies. Flo gives birth, followed by Petra, Ella and Hawkeye during the next week. There are eight pups altogether: Burdock (VWF115), Rhogan Josh (VWM116), Amira (VWF117), Squig (VWF118), Cheriqui (VWF119), Rufus (VWM120), Etosha (VWM121) and Murray (VWM122). Their parentage is not yet certain.
28/01/2007	Rocket Dog becomes the dominant female of Whiskers.

PUBLICATIONS OF THE MEERKAT PROJECT

1998

Clutton-Brock, T.H., Brotherton, P.N.M., Smith, R., McIlrath, G.M., Kansky, R., Gaynor, D., O'Riain, J.M. and Skinner, J.D., 'Infanticide and expulsion of females in a cooperative mammal', *Proceedings of the Royal Society of London* B. 265: 2291–2295.

Clutton-Brock, T.H., Gaynor, D., Kansky, R., MacColl, A.D.C., McIlrath, G., Chadwick, P., Brotherton, P.N.M., O'Riain, J.M., Manser, M. and Skinner, J.D., 'Costs of cooperative behaviour in suricates (Suricata suricatta)', *Proceedings of the Royal Society of London* B. 265: 185–190.

Manser, M.B., 'The evolution of auditory communication in suricates *Suricata suricatta*', PhD thesis: University of Cambridge.

1999

Clutton-Brock, T.H., Gaynor, D., McIlrath, G.M., MacColl, A.D.C., Kansky, R., Chadwick, P., Manser, M., Brotherton, P.N.M. and Skinner, J.D., 'Predation, group size and mortality in a cooperative mongoose, *Suricata suricatta*', *Journal of Animal Ecology* 68: 672–683.

Clutton-Brock, T.H., MacColl, A.D.C., Chadwick, P., Gaynor, D., Kansky, R. and Skinner, J.D., 'Reproduction and survival of suricates *(Suricata suricatta)* in the southern Kalahari', *African Journal of Ecology* 77: 69–80.

Clutton-Brock, T.H., O'Riain, M.J., Brotherton, P.N.M., Gaynor, D., Kansky, R., Griffin, A.S. and Manser, M., 'Selfish sentinels in cooperative mammals', *Science* 284: 1640–1644.

Courchamp, F., Clutton-Brock, T H. & Grenfell, B., 'Inverse density dependence and the Allee effect', *Trends in Ecology & Evolution* 14: 375–415.

Manser, M.B., 'Response of foraging group members to sentinel calls in suricates, *Suricata suricatta'*, *Proceedings of the Royal Society* B. 266: 1013–1019.

2000

Barnard, J.A., 'Costs and benefits of group foraging in cooperatively breeding meerkats', PhD thesis: University of Cambridge.

Clutton-Brock, T.H., Brotherton, P.N.M., O'Riain, M.J., Griffin, A.S., Gaynor, D., Sharpe, L., Kansky, R., Manser, M. and McIlrath, G.M., 'Individual contributions to babysitting in a cooperative mongoose, *Suricata suricatta'*, *Proceedings of the Royal Society* B. 267: 301–305.

Manser, M.B. and Avey, G., 'The effect of pup vocalisations on food allocation in a cooperative mammal, the meerkat (*Suricata suricatta*)', *Behavioural Ecology and Sociobiology* 48: 429–437.

O'Riain, M.J., Bennett, N.C., Brotherton, P.N.M., McIlrath, G.M. and Clutton-Brock, T.H., 'Reproductive suppression and inbreeding avoidance in wild populations of cooperatively breeding meerkats (*Suricata suricatta*)', *Behavioural Ecology and Sociobiology* 48: 471–477.

2001

Brotherton, P.N.M., Clutton-Brock, T.H., O'Riain, M.J., Gaynor, D., Sharpe, L., Kansky, R. and McIlrath, G.M., 'Offspring food allocation by parents and helpers in a cooperative mammal', *Behavioural Ecology* 12: 590–599.

Clutton-Brock, T.H., Brotherton, P.N.M., O'Riain, M.J., Griffin, A.S., Gaynor, D., Kansky, R., Sharpe, L. and McIlrath, G.M., 'Contributions to cooperative rearing in meerkats, *Suricata suricatta'*, *Animal Behaviour* 61: 705–710.

Clutton-Brock, T.H., Brotherton, P.N.M., Russell, A.F., O'Riain, M.J., Gaynor, D., Kansky, R., Griffin, A., Manser, M., Sharpe, L., McIlrath, G.M., Small, T., Moss, A. and Monfort, S., 'Cooperation, conflict and concession in meerkat groups', *Science* 291: 478–481.

Clutton-Brock, T.H., Russell, A.F., Brotherton, P.N.M., Sharpe, L., McIlrath, G.M., White, S. and Cameron, E.Z., 'Effects of helpers on juvenile development and survival in meerkats', *Science* 293: 2446–2449.

Manser, M.B., 'The acoustic structure of suricates' alarm calls varies with predator type and the level of response urgency', *Proceedings of the Royal Society* B. 268: 2315–2324.

Manser, M.B., Bell, M.B. and Fletcher, L.B., 'The information that receivers extract from alarm calls in suricates', *Proceedings of the Royal Society* B. 268: 2485–2491.

Moss, A.M., Clutton-Brock, T.H. and Monfort, S.L., 'Longitudinal gonadal steroid excretion in free-living male and female meerkats (*Suricata suricatta*)', *General and Comparative Endocrinology* 122: 158–171.

White, S.M., 'Juvenile development and conflicts of interest in meerkats', PhD thesis: University of Cambridge.

2002

Clutton-Brock, T.H., 'Meerkats stand tall', *National Geographic Magazine* 52–73.

Clutton-Brock, T.H., Russell, A.F., Sharpe, L.L., Young, A.J., Balmforth, Z. and McIlrath, G.M., Evolution and development of sex differences in cooperative behavior in meerkats', *Science* 297: 253–256.

Manser, M.B., Seyfarth, R.M. and Cheney, D.L., 'Suricate alarm calls signal predator class and urgency', *TRENDS in Cognitive Sciences* 6: 55–57.

Russell, A.F., Clutton-Brock, T.H., Brotherton, P.N.M., Sharpe, L.L., McIlrath, G.M., Dalerum, F.D., Cameron, E.Z. and Barnard, J.A., 'Factors affecting pup growth and survival in cooperatively breeding meerkats *Suricata suricatta*', *Journal of Animal Ecology* 71: 700–709.

Sharpe, L.L., Clutton-Brock, T.H., Brotherton, P.N.M., Cameron, E.Z. and Cherry, M.I., Experimental provisioning increases play in free-ranging meerkats', *Animal Behaviour* 64: 113–121.

Scantlebury, M., Russell, A.F., McIlrath, G.M., Speakman, J.R. and Clutton-Brock, T.H., 'The energetics of lactation in cooperatively breeding meerkats *Suricata suricatta*', *Proceedings of the Royal Society* B. 269: 2147–2153.

2003

Carlson, A.A., Nicol, L., Young, A.J., Parlow, Al.F. and McNeilly, A.S., 'Radioim-munoassay of prolactin for the meerkat (*Suricata suricatta*), a cooperatively breeding carnivore', *General and Comparative Endocrinology* 130: 148–156.

Clutton-Brock, T.H., Russell, A.F. and Sharpe, L.L., 'Meerkat helpers do not specialise in particular activities', *Animal Behaviour* 66: 531–540.

Griffin, A.S., Pemberton, J.M., Brotherton, P.N.M., McIlrath, G.M., Gaynor, D., Kansky, R. and Clutton-Brock, T.H., 'A genetic analysis of breeding success in the cooperative meerkat (*Suricata suricatta*)', *Behavioral Ecology* 14: 472–480.

Russell, A.F., Brotherton, P.N.M., McIlrath, G.M., Sharpe, L.L. and Clutton-Brock, T.H., 'Breeding success in cooperative meerkats: effects of helper number and maternal state', *Behavioural Ecology* 14: 486–492.

Russell, A.F., Sharpe, L.L., Brotherton, P.N.M. and Clutton-Brock, T.H., 'Cost minimization by helpers in cooperative vertebrates', *Proceedings of the National Academy of Sciences (U.S.)* 100: 3333–3338.

Sharpe, L.L. and Cherry, M.I., 'Social play does not reduce aggression in wild meerkats', *Animal Behaviour* 66: 989–997.

Young, A.J., 'Subordinate tactics in cooperative meerkats: breeding, helping and dispersal', PhD thesis: University of Cambridge.

2004

Carlson, A.A., Young, A.J., Russell, A.F., Bennett, N.C., McNeilly, A.S. and Clutton-Brock, T H., 'Hormonal correlates of dominance in meerkats (*Suricata suricatta*)', *Hormones and Behavior* 46: 141–150.

Clutton-Brock, T.H., Russell, A.F. and Sharpe, L.L., 'Behavioural tactics of breeders in cooperative meerkats', *Animal Behaviour* 68: 1029–1040.

Manser, M.B. and Bell, M.B., 'Spatial representation of shelter locations in meerkats (*Suricata suricatta*)', *Animal Behaviour* 68: 151–157.

Manser, M.B. and Fletcher, L.B., 'Vocalise to localise – A test on functionally referential alarm calls', *Interaction Studies* 5: 325–342.

Russell, A.F., Carlson, A.A., McIlrath, G.M., Jordan, N.R. and Clutton-Brock, T.H., 'Adaptive size modification by dominant female meerkats', *Evolution* 58: 1600–1607.

Sharpe, L.L., 'Play and social relationships in the meerkat *Suricata suricatta*', PhD thesis: University of Stellenbosch.

2005

Clutton-Brock, T.H., Russell, A.F., Sharpe, L.L. and Jordan, N.R., '"False-feeding" and aggression in meerkat societies', *Animal Behaviour* 69: 1273–1284.

Hollén, L. and Manser, M.B., 'Studying alarm call communication in meerkats', *Cognition, Brain, Behaviour* Vol. IX(3): 525–538.

Sharpe, L.L., 'Play fighting does not affect subsequent fighting success in wild meerkats', *Animal Behaviour* 69: 1023–1029.

Sharpe, L.L., 'Play does not enhance social cohesion in a cooperative mammal', *Animal Behaviour* 70: 551–558.

Sharpe, L.L., 'Frequency of social play does not affect dispersal partnerships in wild meerkats', *Animal Behaviour* 70: 559–569.

Stephens, P.A., Russell, A.F., Young, A.J., Sutherland, W.J. and Clutton-Brock, T.H., 'Dispersal, eviction and conflict in meerkats (*Suricata suricatta*): An evolutionarily stable strategy model', *American Naturalist* 165: 120–135.

Young, A.J., Carlson, A.A. and Clutton-Brock, T.H., 'Trade-offs between extra-territorial prospecting and helping in a cooperative mammal', *Animal Behaviour* 70: 829–837.

2006

Carlson, A.A., Manser, M.B., Young, A.J., Russell, A.F., Jordan, N.R., McNeilly, A.S. and Clutton-Brock, T.H., 'Cortisol levels are positively associated with pup-feeding rates in male meerkats', *Proceedings of the Royal Society* B 273: 571–577.

Carlson, A.A., Russell, A.F., Young, A.J., Jordan, N.R., McNeilly, A.S., Parlow, Al F. and Clutton-Brock, T.H., 'Elevated prolactin levels immediately precede decisions to babysit by male meerkat helpers', *Hormones and Behavior* 50: 94–100.

Clutton-Brock, T.H., Hodge, S.J., Spong, G., Russell, A.F., Jordan, N.R., Bennett, N.C. and Manser, M.M., 'Intrasexual competition and sexual selection in cooperative meerkats', *Nature* 444: 1065–1068.

Hollén, L.I., 'Development of alarm-call production, usage and responses in meerkats (*Suricata suricatta*)', PhD thesis: Universität Zurich.

Hollén, L.I. and Manser, M.B., 'Ontogeny of alarm call responses in meerkats, *Suricata suricatta*: the roles of age, sex and nearby conspecifics', *Animal Behaviour* 72: 1345–1353.

Kutsukake, N. and Clutton-Brock, T.H., 'Aggression and submission reflect reproductive conflict between females in cooperatively breeding meerkats *Suricata suricatta*', *Behavioral Ecology and Sociobiology* 59: 541–548.

Kutsukake, N. and Clutton-Brock, T.H., 'Social function of allo-grooming in cooperatively breeding meerkats *Suricata suricatta*', *Animal Behaviour* 72: 1059–1068.

Schibler, F.J., 'The irrelevance of individual recognition in meerkats' alarm calls', PhD thesis: Fakultät der Universität Bern.

Stütz, A., 'Acoustic correlates of behavioural arousal in meerkat (*Suricata suricatta*) vocalisations', PhD thesis: Universität Zurich.

Thornton, A. and Mcauliffe, K., 'Teaching in wild meerkats', *Science* 313: 227–229.

Turbé, A., 'Habitat use, ranging behaviour and social control in meerkats', PhD thesis: University of Cambridge.

Young, A.J., Carlson, A.A., Monfort, S.L., Russell, A.F., Bennett, N.C. and Clutton-Brock, T.H., 'Stress and the suppression of subordinate reproduction in cooperatively breeding meerkats', *Proceedings of the National Academy of Sciences (U.S.)* 103: 12005–12010.

Young, A.J. and Clutton-Brock, T., 'Infanticide by subordinates influences reproductive sharing in cooperatively breeding meerkats', *Biology Letters* 2: 385–387

2007

Clutton-Brock, T.H., 'Sexual selection in males and females', *Science* 318: 1882–1885.

Dalerum, F., Bennett, N.C. and Clutton-Brock, T.H., 'Longitudinal differences in 15N between mothers and offspring during and after weaning in a small cooperative mammal, the meerkat (*Suricata suricatta*)', *Rapid Communications in Mass Spectrometry* 21: 1889–1892.

Graw, B. and Manser, M.B., 'The function of mobbing in cooperative meerkats', *Animal Behaviour* 74: 507–517.

Hodge, S.J., Flower, T.P. and Clutton-Brock, T.H., 'Offspring competition and helper associations in cooperative meerkats', *Animal Behaviour* 74: 957–964.

Hollén, L.I. and Manser, M.B., 'Motivation before meaning: motivational information encoded in meerkat alarm calls develops earlier than referential information', *American Naturalist* 169: 758–767.

Hollén, L.I. and Manser, M.B., 'Persistence of alarm-call behaviour in the absence of predators: a comparison between wild and captive-born meerkats (*Suricata suricatta*)', *Ethology* 113: 1038–1047.

Jordan, N., 'Scent-marking investment is determined by sex and breeding status in meerkats' *Animal Behaviour* 74: 531–540.

Jordan, N.R., Cherry, M.I. and Manser, M.B., 'Latrine distribution and patterns of use by wild meerkats: implications for territory and mate defence', *Animal Behaviour* 73: 613–622.

Kunc, H.J., Madden, J.R. and Manser, M.B., 'Begging signals in a mobile feeding system: the evolution of different call types', *American Naturalist* 170: 617–624.

Ross-Gillespie, A. and Griffin, A.S., 'Quick guide: Meerkats', *Current Biology* 17–12, R442.

Russell, A. F., Young, A. J., Spong, G, Jordan, N. R. and Clutton-Brock, T. H., 'Helpers increase the reproductive potential of offspring in cooperative meerkats', *Proceedings of the Royal Society* B. 217: 513–524.

Schibler, F. and Manser, M.B., 'The irrelevance of individual discrimination in meerkat alarm calls', *Animal Behaviour* 74: 1259–1268.

Young, A. J., Spong, A. J., & Clutton-Brock, T. H., 'Subordinate males prospect for extra-group paternity: alternative reproductive tactics in a cooperative mammal', *Proceedings of the Royal Society* B 274: 1603–1609.

2008

Golabek, K.A., Jordan, N.R. and Clutton-Brock, T.H., 'Radiocollars do not affect the survival or foraging behaviour of wild meerkats', *Journal of Zoology* 274: 248–253.

Hodge, S.J., Manica, A., Flower, T.P. and Clutton-Brock, T.H., 'Determinants of reproductive success in dominant female meerkats', *Journal of Animal Ecology* 77: 92–102.

Hollén, L.I., Clutton-Brock, T. and Manser, M.B., 'Ontogenetic changes in alarm-call production and usage in meerkats (*Suricata suricatta*): adaptations or constraints?' *Behavioral Ecology and Sociobiology* 62: 821–829.

Kutsukake, N. and Clutton-Brock, T.H., 'The number of subordinates moderates intrasexual competition among males in cooperatively breeding meerkats', *Proceedings of the Royal Society* B *Biological Sciences* 275: 209–216.

Thornton, A., 'Early body condition, time budgets and the acquisition of foraging skills in meerkats', *Animal Behaviour* 75: 951–962.

ACKNOWLEDGEMENTS

Throughout its fourteen years, the Kalahari Meerkat Project has been the work of a large and varied team. John Skinner, director of the Mammalian Research Institute of the University of Pretoria, played a crucial role in helping us establish the project in the first place and has been a staunch ally and generous host over the whole life of the project. Without his help and guidance our work would have withered and died in the early stages. His successors as director of the institute, Johan du Toit and Elissa Cameron, have been equally helpful, and we are extremely grateful to them. Martin Haupt told us which cars to buy and which to avoid, helped organise our radios and receivers, chased up our licences and took charge of freezing (and later shipping) large quantities of fecal, urine and blood samples. Without Martin's help, we would not have weathered the many logistical storms that we encountered at different stages. Nigel Bennett collaborated with us on our endocrinological studies and carried out most of the analysis of blood samples. His unflagging enthusiasm for all things reproductive lured us down physiological paths we would not otherwise have dared to tread. Steve Monfort of the Smithsonian Institute, international supremo of the fecal sample, helped sort out the techniques for identifying meerkat hormone levels in urine and faeces, organised the analysis of many samples and generously provided us with access to his laboratory.

I am also grateful to the South African National Parks and their staff in Pretoria, Kimberly and the Kgalagadi Transfrontier Park (then the Kalahari Gemsbok National Park) for permission to work in the Park between 1993 and 2001 and for generous hospitality, help and support. During our years in the park we were encouraged, guided and corrected by Mike Knights, Peter Novellie, Anthony Hall-Martin, Elias LeRiche, Gill de Kock and Dries Engelbrecht. Fieldwork in the Park was started by Peter Chadwick, who habituated the first groups and laid the foundation for our work over the next seven years. Subsequently, the work there was run by Andrew MacColl, Peter Brotherton, Marta Manser, David Gaynor, Ruth Kansky and Justin O'Riain, with the help of a number of volunteers including Henry Nicholls, Lawrence Postgate, Kerry McKay, Paul Dixon, Catriona McLeod, Alex Toole, Catriona MacCallum, Sandy Slater-Jones, Kate Parker, Mike Peterson, Sam Clarke, Rebecca Tait and Paul Elsmeere. Daleen Ras, camp manager at Nossob camp, proved invaluable with handling the logistics of running a remote field station.

Research at Rus und Vrede (then the Ranch, now the Kuruman River Reserve) began in 1993 and still continues. We owe an enormous debt to Hennie Kotze, his wife, the late Jeanette Kotze, and their son Johnny Kotze, who allowed us to work on their land, provided us with accommodation (and, later, sold part of their farm to us), helped us to mend our cars and equipment and showed us how to cope with life in the Kalahari. We are grateful to our neighbours at Van Zylsrus for permission to follow meerkats on their land and for their tolerance and support. They include Kleinman Coetze, Jaques Robertze and Philip de Brain.

Research at the ranch was started by Olivia Forge, Collin Britten,

Andre and Gerthe Marais and Grant McIlrath, who located the first groups and learned to identify the first individuals. Grant then worked on the project for the next seven years, honing his skills in habituating meerkats and laying the foundation of our later work. Meerkat groups were initially much wilder on the ranch than in the Park and we were beginning to despair of being able to walk with them when, by dint of great skill and persever-ance, Grant habituated the first group, Avatar – the predecessor of Lazuli. Grant then played a crucial role in habituating other groups and developing techniques of capture before leaving us to start his own independent study of meerkats and other small mammals in the Cape. Marta Manser, Lynda Sharpe, Sarah Davies and Andrew Turner all played an important part in increasing the number of habituated groups.

Many people have been crucial to our work on meerkats on the ranch. I owe much to Marta Manser, who worked with the project as a PhD student, post doc and lately as an independent professor. For the last five years, Marta has co-directed the project and been party to all major decisions. I owe much to her determination, insight and commitment as well as to her skill in identifying opportunities and problems. I am also grateful to her students and colleagues at Zurich who made the six months that Dafila and I spent working with them such an enjoyable time. Lynda Sharpe extended the habituation of groups, focused the work on individ-ual behaviour and played a crucial role in the project for more than eight years; several generations of volunteers have looked to her for guidance, advice and inspiration. Elissa Cameron and Wayne Linklater succeeded her as project managers, stimulating volunteers and students and guiding the project into calmer waters after two tragic accidents. Andy Young and Anne and Ron Carlson followed, sharpening our data collection and analysis and helping us to improve the organisation of many different aspects of the work. For the next two years, the project was run by Neil Jordan, who presided over a period when the project expanded, metamorphosing into the small research village that exists today, and played a key role in establishing the current regime of data collection and long-term experiments. Neil's hard work, dedication and organisation were of crucial importance during the project expansion. Neil was succeeded by Tom Flower, the other Flower of the Kalahari, whose infectious enthusiasm and interest in all things biological sustained everyone who worked with the animals. In preparing this book, I owe much to the help of Tom, who extracted the life histories of members of the Whiskers group from our records and embellished and interpreted them for me. In addition, he played an important part in guiding the filmmakers during the production of the television series.

Over the years, seven technicians have helped to support the scientific work, collaring animals, building houses, repairing roads, keeping our water running and arranging supplies: Johan Fourie, Ron Carlson, Mark Tarrant, Marius van der Merver, Fred Dalerum, Adin Ross-Gillespie and Andre van Wyk. In addition, our work has been supported by the help of Israel Olyn, Hendrik Stephen and Alta Kooper and Ben and Tina Olin.

Twenty-two MSc and PhD students have worked on the project. They include: Jonathan Barnard, Christophe Bousquet, Sinead English, Roman Furrer, Satu Glaser, Beke Graw, Anna Gsell, Linda Hollen, Neil Jordan, Raphaela Lienert, Marta Manser, Maria Rasmussen, Michaela Ruffner, Fabian Schibler, Lynda Sharpe, Angela Stutz, Mico Tatelovic, Alex Thornton, Ann Turbe, Stuart White and Andy Young. In addition, nine post doctoral fellows have worked with us including Pete Brotherton, Anne Carlson, Sarah Hodge, Joah Madden, Marta Manser, Hansjoerg Kunc, Nobu

Kutsukake, Justin O'Riain, Andy Russell, Mike Scantlebury and Goran Spong.

A large number of volunteers and assistants have worked with us for a year or more, acquiring an astonishing level of skill in locating and recognising meerkats, juggling two or even three hand-held computers at the same time, persuading meerkats to get on (and off) the scales and collecting many different types of data. They include: Dave Allsop, Greg Avey, Martyn Baker, Fiona Ballantyne, Zoe Balmforth, Helena Banyard-Smith, Marie-France Barrette, Matt Bell, Dave Bell, Emily Bennitt, Katherine Bradley, Henry Brink, Sandy Crichton, Liz Cattini, Sam Clarke, Lorna Culverwell, Zanna Clay, Sophie Conway, Fred Dalerum, Cyrus Dar, Maeva Devas, Simon Davies, Audrey Detouef-Boulade, Nick Dyer, Salomi Enslin, Yuval Erlich, Mike Finnie, Lindsay Fletcher, Tom Flower, Zoe Fry, Hannah Freeman, Jo Garner, Alison Geldart, Kelly Gill, Alena Gsell, Krystyna Golabek, Chris Gordon, Nicky Green, Helen Hedworth, Marla Hill, Sarah Hodge, Zoe Hodgson, Suzi Hogg, Linda Hollen, Maria Hönig, Cath Hughes, David Jansen, Helen Johnson, Neil Jordan, Andrew King, Sophie Lanfear, Katharina Lederle, Tom Maddox, Rafael Mares, Katie McAulliffe, Dillon McGarry, Julie Merryweather, Bonnie Metherell, Pete Minting, Kelly Moyes, Corsin Muller, Matthew Munchow, Claire Murphy, Anjeli Nathan, Martha Nelson, Henry Nichols, Danny Pezzato, George Potter, Mike Raimondo, Marie Rawlinson, Melinda Ridgway, Kerri-lyn Roelofse, Rebecca Rose, Adin Ross-Gillespie, Kristin Schüring, Adam Seward, Mike Sheehan, Kirsten Skinner, Rebecca Smith, Ruth Snelson, Anne Sommerfield, Rowena Staff, Joel Stibbard, Andy Sully, Robert Sutcliffe, Rebecca Tait, Mark Tarrant, Iain Taylor, Lindsey Taylor, Gill Telford, Ben Themen, Sandra Tranquilli, Kristina Turner, Russell Venn, Saritha Visvalingham, Helen Wade, Caroline Walker, Kevin Wallace,

Hugh Webster, Dom Wright, Jessica Wright and Richard Yarnell. Without our team of volunteers our work would not have been possible and I would have had no story to tell.

During the course of the project, two volunteers, Ben Themen and Anjeli Nathan, both outstanding students and remarkable people, were killed in separate car crashes. At a time of great loss, both their parents showed great generosity and enormous kindness in helping us cope with the tragedy at a time of great distress, and I shall continue to be grateful to them for the rest of my life.

Over the last few years, volunteers for the Earthwatch Institute have also played an important role in helping us to follow groups and collect information on the animals and their environment. The Earthwatch teams have been run by Adin Ross-Gillespie, Anne-Marie Stuart and Helene Brettschneider. I am also grateful to the Earthwatch Institute and their staff for their support. In addition, Aliza Le Roux studied yellow mongooses on the reserve while Mandy Ridley, Andy Radford, Nichola Raihani, Martha Nelson and Krystyna Golabek worked on babblers and contributed much to our understanding of differences and similarities between mammals and birds.

Our work on meerkats has been funded principally by the British Natural Environment Research Council (NERC) and the Biology and Biotechnology Research Council (BBSRC). In addition, the work of Marta Manser's students and post docs has been funded by the Swiss National Science Foundation. For assistance in purchasing and maintaining the ranch we are indebted to the Newton Fund Trust, the Balfour Trust, the Bryan Guinness Charitable Trust, the Ernest Kleinwort Charitable Trust and the Netherlands Foundation for International Nature Conservation (the Van Tienhoven Foundation).

Analysis of genetic samples (which has made it possible to

identify which males fathered which pups) has been master-minded by Josephine Pemberton and Ashleigh Griffin from the University of Edinburgh and by Goran Spong in Uppsala.

In Cambridge, Pete Brotherton, Andyman Russell and Sarah Hodge worked as the principal post docs, leading the analysis of our increasingly large dataset, producing papers, selecting volunteers and leading the management of the work. They have been vital to the organisation and success of the project, working with me to produce many of the scientific papers that have come out of our research, providing ideas and numerical expertise, directing research in the field and coping with the logistical problems of maintaining a large field team at a very isolated site. Over the last three years, Sarah Hodge has been the unruffleable anchorwoman of the project, selecting volunteers, organising the numerical analyses and coping calmly with crises and catastrophes, tantrums and occasional euphoria. I am immensely grateful to all three of them.

Penny Roth, my long-standing secretary, has helped to organise me and the rest of my research group throughout the duration of the project, putting up with successive drafts of my papers in atrocious handwriting, periods of tension and euphoria, and has kept smiling serenely. I am deeply grateful to her. Jo Jones learned to decipher my hieroglyphics and typed two drafts of this book. Her comments helped to clarify many turgid passages and often helped me to sort out my thoughts. Luigi Bonomi, my agent, introduced me to Michael Dover and Peter Dawson, who produced this book – which includes photographs by Andy Young, Joah Madden and Rob Sutcliffe. I am also particularly grateful to Debbie Woska at Orion, who helped me with the final corrections.

I owe a large debt to Caroline Hawkings and Claire Birks at

Oxford Scientific Films, who realised the parallels between human soap operas and the lives of our animals. The three series of Meerkat Manor that they produced broke new ground in wildlife TV, providing accurate insights into the lives of individuals that have not been matched by previous programmes on mammals. Caroline and her successive teams have been a pleasure to work with and have lubricated our life in the Kalahari in several ways.

It is a great pleasure to thank my colleagues at the Department of Zoology in Cambridge for their support, interest and tolerance of protracted absences. They include Malcolm Burrows, Andrew Balmford, Nick Davies, William Foster, Bill Amos, Andrea Manica, Rufus Johnstone, and Becky Kilner. Keith Griffin has kept our computers running and Bill Lee has provided logistical support. Julian Jacobs has kept administration of the project (reasonably) straight and narrow.

Outside Cambridge, I am grateful to many colleagues who advised, counselled, stimulated or guided our work. They are too numerous to name, but I am particularly grateful to David Macdonald, Marta Manser, Scott Creel, Phillip Richardson, Ann Rasa, Tim Jackson, Rosie Woodroffe, Jan Nel, Mike Cherry, Paul Sherman, Paul Harvey, Ben Hatchwell, Craig Packer, Francis Ratnicks, Steve Stearns and Barbara König.

Finally, I am deeply grateful to my family. My wife Dafila Scott has worked with me from the beginning of the project, making fieldwork a joy and providing valuable insights into the behaviour of the animals as well as many striking pictures. My children, Amber and Peter, have travelled with us to the Kalahari and have put up with life in a field camp and many parental obsessions; my mother Eileen has put up with our protracted field trips and long absences.